PROFESSIONAL PAPERS.—FOURTH SERIES.

VOL. I.—No. 4.

ARMOURED TRAINS.

BY

Capt. H. O. MANCE, D.S.O., R.E.

(Lecture delivered at the Royal Engineers Institute on 2nd November, 1905).

PRINTED BY
W. & J. MACKAY & CO,, LTD., CHATHAM.
1400—160. 4. 06.

Published by Books Express Publishing
Copyright © Books Express, 2011
ISBN 978-1-78039-505-0

Books Express publications are available from all good retail and online booksellers. For
publishing proposals and direct ordering please contact us at: info@books-express.com

CONTENTS.

ARMOURED TRAINS.

By Capt. H. O. Mance, D.S.O., R.E.

Prior to the South African War the lack of data based on actual experience rendered it only possible to consider the general subject of armoured trains tentatively ; and even now, owing to the entirely different circumstances and surroundings in which campaigns may be fought, as compared with South African experience, it is only with caution that the application in future warfare of the general principles underlying the employment of armoured trains can be forecasted. In Egypt in 1882 an armoured train, constructed by Capt. Fisher, R.N., was of great use on the reconnaissance of August 5th. Two trucks were armoured with iron plates and sandbags and a Nordenfelt and two Gatling guns were mounted in them, and also a 9-pr. Other armoured trucks contained 200 bluejackets. A 40-pr. gun was also used with great effect from a truck protected by an iron mantlet. The locomotive was placed in the middle of the train and protected by slung sandbags and rails.

The subject may be divided into three main heads :—

I. The Uses of armoured trains, in which will be considered how the essential characteristics of armoured trains can be best turned to account.

II. The Construction, Equipment, and Garrisons of armoured trains, with a view to their undertaking the duties indicated in (1) with a maximum of efficiency.

III. The Organization and Administration of armoured trains and the many details involved in the same.

I. THE USES OF ARMOURED TRAINS.

The particular characteristics of an armoured train (excluding of course heavy guns mounted on railway trucks) are as follows :—

(1). *Very great mobility* in certain definite directions only, and with limitations noted below. This mobility implies :—

  (*a*). *Power to effect concentration* with rapidity, and the possibility therefore of employing every train where it will be of the greatest use.

  (*b*). *Ability to reinforce* threatened points speedily.

(2). *Great strength* (except against guns) both for defence and offence within its radius of action.

(3). *Continuous availability* day and night ; when the engine is being washed out or repaired another can be substituted if necessary.

(4). *Moral effect*, both as a support to co-operating forces and when making a sudden descent on the enemy.

(5). *Comparative freedom from surprise* owing to its always being in fighting formation ; also the advantages gained by a knowledge of the country at least as favourable as that of the enemy.

(6). *No trouble to ration.*

(7). *Liability to have communications interrupted*, and therefore to be isolated with comparative ease ; and also to be destroyed or seriously damaged by skilfully laid mines, etc.

In South Africa, however, the damage to armoured trains by mines was much less than might have been expected. The Boers rarely laid mines at bridges, or even at small culverts, possibly because they imagined the approaches were mined by us, or because they thought that their own mines were likely to be discovered. Thus, the garrisons of the trains, unless actually injured by the explosion, which at most affected one truck, stood a good chance of escaping unhurt, mere derailments not being very dangerous at the speeds employed. Three kinds of efficient mines were laid :—

  (*a*). *Contact mines*, which went off under the first truck. A truck of railway material was pushed ahead to explode any such.

  (*b*). *Contact mines with delay action fuze*, so as to go off a few seconds after the release of the mechanism. The delay action fuze is liable to fail and thus render the mine useless. It is also purely a matter of chance whether the explosion occurs when any particular truck is over the mine ; however, they might do damage.

(c). *Observation mines* let off by a string pulled at the right moment. This was the most dangerous pattern in South Africa, but its employment was discontinued owing to the fact that the man pulling the string had not much chance of getting off. When such mines were expected maxim fire used to be opened on any likely cover for watchers before the train passed it. It will be seen that in no case is a mine in the open likely to render a train completely *hors de combat.* A mine on a bridge or sharp curve on a high bank might do so by wrecking the whole train. It the enemy takes to interfering with the line it is a good thing to mine the approaches to the larger bridges and culverts and spread reports that the whole line is mined ; also to lay ambushes to meet expected raids. If mines are laid, precautions should be taken to protect one's own troops and friendlies.

(8). *Vulnerability to artillery fire.* Experience in South Africa points to the fact that it is not at all easy to hit an armoured train with artillery fire, especially if a well-directed fire is kept up from the guns of the armoured train. A single attacking gun, especially if not well placed, might be overwhelmed, before it had done much damage, by converging fire from two armoured trains. A Russian armoured train appears to have sallied out from Port Arthur and to have been subjected to artillery fire. It managed to return, however, so that the damage could not have been very severe.

(9). *Liability to railway accidents,* especially if the O.C. does not possess the necessary grounding in railway technical knowledge. Most of the armoured train casualties in South Africa were due to railway accidents not caused directly by the enemy.

(10). *The freedom of action* of armoured trains is affected by, and affects, the running of traffic on the railway. Armoured trains must give way to ordinary trains except for urgent military reasons, as otherwise the proper maintenance of traffic, which is one of the objects of armoured trains, would be impeded.

(11). *Expensive to run.* The cost of the engine and trucks, wages of enginemen and guard, coal and stores, must be reckoned with.

USES IN OPEN COUNTRY.

It is hardly likely that any other country will lend itself so extensively to armoured train operations as was the case in South Africa during the campaign of 1899–1902. The area of operations was enormous and the troops available for guarding the great length of the line of communications which had to be protected were small in number. The enemy were devoid of artillery during the greater part of the campaign, and an armoured train, if isolated, could hold

Conditions in South Africa.

out against any force which could be brought to attack it. The enemy were also unenterprising in their attempts to wreck the trains, being disheartened either by complete lack of success or by the insignificant results which seemed to reward their somewhat hazardous raids. Those inhabitants who might have been hostile were removed. The quantity of traffic required to be run was limited, and even on the most important line night running could be dispensed with and the line kept clear for armoured train operations. The open nature of most of the country and the absence of deep cuttings and tunnels afforded a clear field of fire, and together with lower speeds reduced the chance of a railway accident to a minimum.

Duties under Similar Conditions.   Under these and similar circumstances armoured trains can be usefully employed for the following duties :—

(1). *Accompanying extended advance guard cavalry* to forces advancing astride a railway.

(2). *Drawing the fire of the enemy's guns.* This was only done in the earlier stages of the war in South Africa, when the armoured trains were not provided with guns and had to withdraw as soon as their object was effected, *e.g.*, Graspan and Magersfontein.

(3). *Escorting construction trains* at rail-head or when repairing damage to the line effected by the enemy. Later on each armoured train carried enough railway material to repair slight breaks in the railway or telegraph. In the case of breakdown trains, armoured trucks should be provided for the repairing party in case attacked *en route* to the break.

(4). *Patrolling* an otherwise undefended line. If an unguarded line is left to itself for most of the day and night the enemy are encouraged to destroy it frequently. The mere knowledge of an armoured train patrolling the section limits, or prevents, this. To avoid firing on our own patrols orders were issued to all concerned that, if an armoured train signalled to parties near the railway by a wide shot, they were at once to send a man to report and meanwhile were not to move further away from the line, otherwise they would be fired at. This worked very well.

(5). *Escorting Trains* either singly or in convoys of three or even four trains. Even if there are not enough troops to blockhouse the railway, it is possible to ensure a fairly constant and reliable service of trains in spite of the proximity of comparatively large bodies of the enemy, provided the traffic does not exceed three or four trains daily in each direction and the country is open. The general principle of the system employed is to provide each train with sufficient escort to hold out against an attack by any likely number of the enemy until relieved in the ordinary course.

In South Africa, where the trains rarely ran over 30 miles an hour, on the Mafeking railway, the line was divided into sections of 100 to 150 miles between the important garrisoned locomotive centres, these distances being a daylight run. All the trains for the day, not exceeding four, left these centres at daybreak for the next centre in either direction, escorted normally by one armoured train, which ran after the first train ; also one armoured truck with a garrison of 10 men was attached to the rear of each of the last two trains. The trains of a convoy maintained an interval of 400 to 600 yards, with orders if attacked to close up unless otherwise ordered by O.C., Armoured Train, who was responsible for the defence of the convoy. The leading train pushed one or two loaded trucks before it if the existence of mines was suspected. Protection from bullets was provided for the drivers and guards on the more threatened sections. Additional single trains can be run independently if escort is available, or occasionally unescorted trains may be risked if the intelligence obtained is good and the line is not specially threatened. Troop trains were run unescorted, but some armoured trucks were attached for part of the troops to occupy as a *point d'appui* if attacked. If the enemy is reported in force within striking distances of the railway the escort must be strengthened by adding one or more armoured trucks or by running an extra armoured train behind the convoy. As all the trains and trucks employed on the above duty were of the open pattern without overhead cover, it was necessary to hold the few commanding points over the line by blockhouse posts, which also patrolled over unheld broken ground near the railway before the passage of the trains. (The above is only an outline of the scheme which worked very well on the section referred to).

(6). *Reinforcing isolated posts* or a line of blockhouses if attacked, or a small detachment operating near the railway, or a thin line of troops awaiting the enemy driven up to the railway by other troops as in the S. African " drives." In view of the very small garrisons employed, the armoured train was in itself stronger than all but the largest garrisons on the line of communication.

(7). *Lying in wait at night* at likely places in a line of blockhouses, or failing this with a line of outposts along the railway at wide intervals, so as to discover parties of the enemy trying to cross or damage the line, and either drive them back or force them to abandon their cattle, sheep, transport, etc. In this way, by making the act of crossing the railway a risky one, the free movement of parties of the enemy is undoubtedly hampered, and interruptions to the railway are reduced in proportion.

(8). *Escorting platelaying gangs* when individual gangers are sniped and the line has to be maintained by strong gangs working under escort.

(9). *Collecting information from gangers and others* and acting as moving telegraph and telephone offices and signal stations.

(10). *Escorting* special stores such as dynamite, ammunition, heavy guns, etc.

(11). *Escorting* prisoners, or superior officers on inspection duty when the trains are not otherwise employed.

At Mafeking also during the early stages of the siege an armoured train was employed with considerable effect. Owing to the level nature of the country an open pattern armoured truck, with armouring only 4 ft. 6 ins. high, could be employed over large districts and this could be improvised cheaply and quickly.

USES IN ENCLOSED COUNTRY.

Altered Conditions as compared with South Africa.

Circumstances which affect the utility of armoured trains favourably or adversely abound to a far greater extent than might be imagined from the above review of the subject ; and as many of them are of a highly technical nature, a thorough railway as well as a military training is essential for due weight to be given to each factor of the situation. It is proposed for sake of an example to enquire into some of the considerations affecting the possible employment of armoured trains in a close country like England, as it is hoped in this way to bring some of the main principles to light.

The altered *military* considerations, as compared with South Africa, are :—

(a). The limited area of operations in the case of England itself, which might result in the line of communications being so short compared with the front occupied that it is unlikely to require special protection.

In such a case there would be little scope for the special advantages of armoured trains, as, except possibly for coast defence, their *rôle* is almost entirely on the lines of communications.

It is surprising that no mention has been made of armoured trains in Manchuria ; but possibly, owing to the enormous front occupied by the opposing armies, the chances of the communications being effectively attacked by either side were so remote that it was not worth while withdrawing much-needed engines and rolling stock from traffic for armoured train work.

(b). In England also we should be operating in a friendly and densely populated country, where, however, agents of the enemy might be residing in guises difficult to detect among so many aliens.

(c). The country on the whole is very close and wooded so that as a rule the field of fire from the railway is limited. Tunnels, deep cuttings, hedges and fences bounding the railway must be considered. The latter cannot be levelled owing to the danger of cattle on the line (none of the English engines have cow-catchers).

(*d*). Owing to high banks and cuttings the pattern and armament of armoured trains would have to be modified. This point comes more properly under the heading of construction. The method of use is, however, affected directly and indirectly owing to the difficulty of improvising suitable armouring.

(*e*). The garrisons of posts will probably be larger than was the case in South Africa, so that an armoured train would not be of such relative importance as a reinforcement.

(*f*). The enemy may have guns. He will probably be enterprising in his attempts to damage the railway or wreck armoured trains.

(*g*). It may be our duty to attack armoured trains employed by the enemy on captured lines.

(*h*). The special feature arises of employing armoured trains on coast defence.

Among the *railway* considerations are :—

(*a*). Much more and much faster traffic under normal circumstances. The ordinary traffic of the country could doubtless be considerably cut down in the theatre of operations, but would only be replaced by military traffic.

(*b*). This and the speeds employed, even if considerably reduced, and the short distances visible along the line, would very greatly add to the risk of accidents in working armoured trains ; and would demand high·technical qualifications from O.C.s and much stricter regulations for working.

(*c*). The quantity and elaborate nature of engineering works on the railway, the far heavier rail (about 100 lbs. per yard as compared with 60 lbs. in South Africa), and the numerous points and crossings, render it possible for the enemy to effect rapid damage to the line of a more serious nature than in South Africa.

(*d*). The complexity of the signals will necessitate the employment of a driver or a pilot driver who knows the section of the line on which the train happens to be, instead of the same driver sufficing everywhere.

(*e*). There would probably be less difficulty in arranging for the construction of armoured trains than was the case in S. Africa.

From the above it is reasonable to anticipate the following uses for armoured trains or armoured trucks in a close country, the existence of a fairly long line of communications liable to attack being presupposed.

Duties under Enclosed Country Conditions.

(1). *At favourable places for coast defence.* These places would have to be carefully ascertained in peace time, so that the General Staff can at once know whether it is any use employing armoured trains to resist a landing at any spot. It is probable that only the guns of the armoured trains could be brought into action in most cases, but the armoured trains might act as an escort to any larger guns mounted on trucks and employed for coast defence as suggested by Lieut.-Colonel Sir Percy Girouard, K.C.M.G., R.E., some years ago.

(2). *Acting as a support for the advanced guard cavalry* to a force advancing astride of a railway, and to draw fire from the enemy's artillery.

(3). *Effecting minor repairs to the railway,* escorting construction trains, special stores, as already mentioned, prisoners, and superior officers on inspection duty.

(4). *Patrolling* a line of railway, and the country for a certain distance on each side, by sending out scouts at different points and collecting information from all available sources.

(5). *Escorting,* in the manner already detailed, *one* or *two* trains if the country is not too close. Convoys of more than two trains will hardly ever be possible on account of the difficulty in seeing them from the armoured train and consequently of defending them. Armoured protection for the driver and guard and a small escort, the latter in an armoured truck or in an armoured guard's van with provision for flanking fire along the train, will often be necessary to defend otherwise helpless trains from molestation by small parties of the enemy or by lawless bands which might come into existence in time of war. Troops in trains are helpless against surprise unless at least part of them are in armoured trucks. This is more necessary in a close than in an open country.

(6). An armoured train would be valuable as a *support for a strong patrol* sent out swiftly from any point on the railway to act against parties of the enemy or roving bands of hooligans, and might possibly assist in the operations.

(7). An armoured train would be a useful *reinforcement to a weak line of troops* holding a railway, or to a post either before or after an attack at short notice. However, an enterprising enemy would probably cut the line badly on each side of such a post, and possibly lay special traps and ambushes for expected armoured trains ; also, as stated above, the posts being larger an armoured train would not afford such a relatively large reinforcement as was the case in South Africa. Naturally armoured trains cannot reinforce troops posted over tunnels and such positions would have to be held in greater strength in consequence. It might here be suggested that in the altered conditions, certainly the maxims and possibly the guns as well should be provided with alternative portable or mobile mountings besides their fixed ones on the train ; for, when reinforcing troops in a cutting the maxims and some of the rifles would have to be taken to the top of the cutting ; also, if the enemy have guns, it would perhaps be necessary to employ the armament and garrison of the armoured train in the defences of the post reinforced, and not in the train ; and finally, should the train be isolated by a superior force of the enemy it might be possible to abandon it and save the armament.

(8). As *movable telegraph and telephone offices* and signal stations.

It is evident that whereas armoured trains played a very prominent part in the defence of lines of communication in South Africa, and even materially assisted in some of the main operations, in campaigns in a civilised country their *rôle* would be more subordinate, though, if fully utilized for such duties as they are specially fitted for, they would release troops for more useful work elsewhere. Instances would possibly occur where, by seizing a favourable opportunity, the officer commanding an armoured train could inflict severe damage on the enemy ; but at the same time a few disasters due to the enemy or railway accidents may be expected even in the most favourable circumstances. In any future campaign the value of armoured trains will probably lie somewhere between the two extreme cases which have been considered.

II. THE CONSTRUCTION, EQUIPMENT, AND GARRISONS
OF ARMOURED TRAINS.

At the commencement of the South African campaign armoured trains consisted merely of a completely armoured engine and of two trucks with their sides and roof armoured with loopholed $\frac{1}{2}$-in. iron plates; no other accommodation was provided. The garrison was 25 to 30 strong, with two maxims. Having no guns and not being shell proof, the armoured trains had to retire immediately they came within range of the artillery possessed by the Boers. Later on, as a result of the lengthy and varied experience against Boers without guns, the component parts of a regular armoured train in S.A. were as follows (see *Plates* I. and III.) :—

Composition in South African War.

(1). Engine and tender.
(2). Tank truck.
(3). Two armoured trucks, each fitted up for infantry garrison, maxim, and searchlight projector.
(4). Gun truck.
(5). Material truck.
(6). Accommodation for officers and servants.
(7).   „   „ enginemen.
(8).   „   „ telegraph instruments and operators.
(9). Searchlight truck for engine and dynamo and men in charge.
(10). Communications.

These will be considered in order.

In South Africa the armoured trains, even at the best of times, were more or less improvised and consequently separate trucks were often employed for officers, enginemen, telegraph and dynamo, thus making a very long train. In civilized countries, if armoured trains were designed in peace time, these might all be provided for in one long coach body, which could be armoured and used as a fighting truck by the details occupying it. Similarly a gun might be mounted in each of the maxim trucks, thereby reducing the number of trucks to three, besides the engine, tank if required, and material truck. A material truck might be placed at each end of the train to save shunting. The above arrangement reduces the amount of armouring required and may perhaps render protected communication along the train possible. Whether a 12-pr. gun would too seriously interfere with the infantry and maxim fire on the same truck would require to be tested by experiment. A 6-pr. gun so mounted caused no prohibitive inconvenience in South Africa.

The separation of the fighting parts of an armoured train by unarmoured trucks, for the close defence of which only a limited amount of flanking fire was provided, presented no serious disadvantages in an open country like South Africa, under conditions where an actual assault on an armoured train was never undertaken ; but in a close country, with a daring civilised enemy, or in savage warfare, the contingency of an assault will have to be provided for. Obviously a more compactly designed train, armoured throughout as suggested above, and with adequate flanking fire, would be less vulnerable ; but, in addition, attention would have to be directed to the advisability of introducing the use of obstacles, which may be of two classes :—(a) Portable obstacles to be employed a short distance from the train to stop a rush ; (b) barbed wire or other screens, either permanently fixed on the train or arranged to let down when required, so as to prevent the enemy from crawling under or between trucks or (in the case of open pattern trucks) from climbing up the sides.

(1). ENGINE AND TENDER.

At the end of the war it was only considered necessary to armour the cab of the engine and a few of the more vulnerable parts such as the injector pipes, the boiler being bullet proof. It is preferable to armour the tender so as to give the train a small assured supply of water for manœuvring under fire ; but this was often dispensed with, as any holes could be easily stopped by wood plugs kept in readiness if the bullet penetrated (which it usually failed ·to do if it struck the tender below the water level). If it came to the very worst the fires could be drawn after the armoured train had stopped in a good tactical position, where it could hold out for as long as necessary. The effect of modern rifle fire at close range on the boiler, engine, and tender might with advantage be experimented with as, in view of the possibility, under other conditions, of fire being opened at point blank range, it may be found necessary to armour the whole of the engine as in the early South African pattern.

The doors of the armoured cab should slide open or, failing this, open inwards. Doors opening outwards are liable to foul fixed structures—a most important point to guard against for all parts of the train. Also doors are often opened and made fast by drivers while running, in spite of orders, and those opening outwards cannot be closed in a hurry in the event of the enemy suddenly firing on a train. (A fireman was killed owing to this cause on an armoured train near Houtkraal in December, 1900. Had the driver also been hit a disaster would have resulted as there was only one set of enginemen on the train at the time).

A good noiseless engine with a large reserve of power should be chosen as it has to work under disadvantageous conditions of varying

water and fuel, starting at short notice and with irregular and sometimes long periods between washouts.   One spare engine for every
five armoured trains should be available to facilitate repairs, washouts,
etc.   This can be employed on shunting in the meanwhile.

(2). TANK TRUCKS.

These are required where the locomotive water supply is not at
frequent intervals.   In S.A. two or even three were occasionally used.
The tank is not usually armoured, nor is it necessarily a fixture on
the train, as it is often convenient to shunt it off when empty and
replace it by a full tank.   It should have a flexible coupling with the
tender ; but in case of a difference of level between the floors of the
tank truck and tender, each armoured train should carry a lift and force
pump and sufficient hose to pump from the tank to the tender and
even from a reservoir on the ground level to the tender.   In waterless
countries provision should be made for an adequate supply of suitable
tank trucks from the commencement.

(3). MAXIM TRUCKS.

One of these is situated at each end of the train (except when there
is a material truck).   A maxim is mounted at one end of the truck in
such a way as to give practically all-round fire.   The remainder of the
truck is loopholed for the infantry escort.   Bogie trucks were usually
employed on account of the increased accommodation.   Provision
should be made for an extra maxim, carried as a spare, to be brought
into action, and armoured protection must be provided for a searchlight projector close to and above the end maxim.

Maxim trucks and armoured trucks for infantry escorts may be
broadly divided into two patterns ;—the *closed pattern* with armoured
roof, for use in hilly countries or where the train is liable to plunging
fire (possibly also with armoured floor where high embankments are
to be run over), and the *open pattern*, for use in open countries where
sufficient cover is afforded by armouring 4 ft. 6 ins. to 5 ft. high.

The *closed pattern* truck in South Africa was invariably armoured
with steel or iron plates, and being of elaborate construction required
a large amount of skilled labour and could not be improvised.
Provision was usually made for flanking fire.   *Open pattern* trucks
could be armoured with either plate, rails, shingle between
corrugated iron or boards, Jarrah sleepers, etc. ; the sides being low
and not required to support a heavy roof, it is comparatively easy to
improvise such trucks.   For temporary purposes large iron plates
laid across the sides of an open truck will give protection from plunging fire except for the maxim detachment.

Steel plate is undoubtedly the best material for armouring as there
are no weak joints and the loopholes can be made smaller than with

any other pattern armouring for the same field of fire ; moreover plates are absolutely bullet proof up to the edges of the holes if $\frac{1}{2}$-in. steel or iron is used. Such loopholes can also have sliding doors to close them when not in use or to vary their size according to circumstances. In close countries the question of loopholes, both for the infantry and also for the gun and maxims, is of great importance, for the train may be attacked at point-blank range and by troops who are under cover themselves. In these circumstances, assuming equally good troops on both sides, the advantage lies with the side present-ing the least vulnerable target ; an armoured train with small steel loopholes would be more favourably situated than the attackers in this respect, and could therefore hold its own against a considerably larger body of opponents. The more open the country the greater the relative strength of an armoured train and the less important to have elaborate armouring or small loopholes.

In plate armoured *closed pattern* trucks (*Plate* I.) the maxim is Closed mounted in a barbette, armoured to a height of 3 ft. and situated at Pattern. the end of the truck and cut off from the rest of the truck by transverse armoured plates provided with means of access to the barbette. (The maxim must have an efficient shield and a mounting capable of firing over the ends or sides of the truck). The side and end armouring of the barbette is again carried on from a height of 5 ft. to the roof of the truck, thus giving cover to the man working the search light which is fixed immediately over the maxim in this pattern truck. The projector is mounted on the roof and the head and shoulders of the man working it emerge through a manhole and are protected as far as possible by hinged plates. Side ports, about 15 ins. square, with sliding doors, are necessary in at least one of the two maxim trucks for the spare maxim. It should be possible for the O.C. to control the train both from the barbette and from the infantry part of the truck.

In the case of *open pattern* trucks in South Africa (*Plate* III.), the Open Pattern. maxim was usually mounted *en barbette* firing over the top of the truck armouring, the tripod mounting being usually employed. In one case the maxim was mounted in a revolving turret, thus giving complete protection (*Fig.* 1, *Plate* II.). In all mountings a shield is absolutely necessary ; the porthole is a death trap without one. If made locally the minimum thickness of steel for the shield should be $\frac{3}{8}$ in., better $\frac{1}{2}$ in. The holes or slots in the maxim brackets for attaching the shields were found to vary considerably in the numerous patterns met with, and as this may occur again a rubbing of the bracket should invariably be sent with any requisition for a shield. It might be possible to design for the maxim and firer an all-round shield, about 18 ins. deep, fixed to a strengthened maxim mounting somewhat in the way that the present shield is fixed, and turning with the maxim ; this would give as good cover as an expensive turret. Weight could be reduced by using specially hardened steel, in which case possibly $\frac{1}{8}$ to $\frac{1}{4}$ of an inch would suffice.

A special reserve of water for the maxim must be provided and kept where it cannot be misappropriated.

As mentioned before extra mobile or portable mountings may be advisable under certain circumstances. The ordinary tripod mounting, as generally used in South Africa, is probably sufficiently portable for the purpose, but a light wheeled mounting with space for boxes of ammunition would be better.

Among other mountings used on armoured trains one may mention a mounting consisting of one leg and two hooks, the latter to engage on the sides of the truck. This was sometimes used for the type of closed armoured trucks described above. Maxims were raked up from all sources for use on armoured trains. On No. 11 armoured train, originally constructed at Buluwayo in 1899, there was a ·450 maxim firing black powder. The mounting consisted of a travelling body minus the wheels, supported at the right height above the floor of the truck. As may be imagined the axles were very much in the way until a more convenient mounting was substituted. This train was sometimes called the cuttle-fish on account of its habit of obscuring itself in its own smoke when attacked. Other maxims were supplied without mountings or with equally inconvenient ones for armoured train purposes, and special mountings had to be designed for them. In some cases maxims could slide on rails across the truck and fire over either side if required.

The chief point is to mount the maxim so as to have the largest possible field of fire and ample elevation and depression, and so that it can be expeditiously worked without the firer unnecessarily exposing himself. The question of elevation is particularly important in the case of portholes ; in one case a maxim was fixed at such a height that it could not be aimed at an elevation over 600 yards. Major-General Sir E. Hutton has suggested that each maxim should have a universal joint to make it independent of the inclination of the truck. This would be an important improvement if it can be devised, especially in the case of a derailed truck. 10,000 rounds per maxim were carried (3,000 in belts) and 300 rounds per rifle ; also a complete box of spare parts for each maxim.

Search Light.   The search light in these open trucks is best mounted in a conning-tower built immediately behind the maxim and thus giving it some protection (*Plate* III.). The floor of this tower rests on the top of the armouring, 4 ft. 6 ins. to 5 ft. above the floor of the truck. The tower is armoured with plates 3 ft. high and is made about 6 ft. long and the width of the truck. It should be accessible both by a trap-door and by ladders outside. The projector and also all the means of controlling the train are placed in this conning-tower, which holds three or four people and should have a few small loopholes 6 ins. from the top of the armouring.

The infantry part of the truck is loopholed 3 ft. from the floor, for Infantry. firing, sitting, or kneeling. Loopholes may be provided at the corners or ends for flanking fire, if not otherwise arranged for. These trucks are usually roofed in with a low wooden or canvas awning with flaps to let down in case of rain. They are healthier than closed trucks in warm dry climates. In all maxim and infantry trucks for use on armoured trains provision should be made for easy access to the truck ; also for cooking, as this would have to be done on the train ; and possibly it may be advisable to arrange a minimum of latrine accommodation, so that the garrison may have no excuse for leaving the train when they are likely to be required at a moment's notice. A 200-gallon tank for drinking water should be fixed in each truck.

(4). GUN TRUCK.

The guns employed latterly on armoured trains in South Africa were the pompom, 3-pr., 6-pr., and 12-pr. Q.F. on cone mountings. There were also a few obsolete weapons which need not be considered.

An excellent description with drawings and photos of the arrangement of a 12-pr. Q.F. on a truck (*Plate* IV.) is given in the *Detailed History of the Railways in South Africa*, recently published by the R.E. Institute, and it is unnecessary to repeat it here. The main points are the necessity of blast-proof magazines if all-round fire is required ; the provision of armoured protection for the crew against frontal, enfilade, and reverse fire, and if necessary plunging fire ; the necessity for very firmly bolting down the pedestal and the mounting of the gun to the framework of the truck, and at the same time for distributing the shock all over the frame of the truck. Sufficient depression and elevation must be allowed for to meet every contingency.

The small guns were similarly mounted in short trucks but without blast-proof magazines (see *Plate* V.). The ammunition carried consisted of 200 rounds per 12-pr. (50 % shrapnel, 30 % common, and 20 % case), 300 rounds per 6-pr. and 3-pr., and 3,000 rounds per Pompom. The feasibility of hand-drawn mobile mountings for guns on armoured trains was not tried in South Africa.

(5). MATERIAL TRUCK.

The material truck, pushed in front of the train to explode contact mines and therefore known as the " spasms " truck, consisted in South Africa of an ordinary bogie truck containing a supply of railway and telegraph material and breakdown appliances for temporary and small repairs. A strong cow-catcher was fixed to each end of this truck and was the means of averting many accidents. The rails and sleepers may be arranged as armouring in the manner described below (page 22), thus giving more space and some extra protected accommodation which might be useful on occasion.

(6). OFFICERS' ACCOMMODATION.

There will always be two officers on a train; three would be necessary in the case of more elaborate trains in civilized warfare if a day and night service is to be maintained. Continued life on a moving train, without other exercise, subsisting largely on tinned food, long and very irregular hours, and tiring exposure when in front of the train in wet or cold weather, let alone periods of anxiety, make the life of an armoured train officer a hard one, as was proved by the nervous and physical breakdowns in the case of several officers so employed in the late war.

Being possible under the circumstances, a certain standard of comfort should be aimed at in regard to accommodation for officers on armoured trains (and for the men also for that matter) to minimise the disadvantages referred to and to increase indirectly the efficiency of the train. A small kitchen, with accommodation for one servant therein, should be arranged for; also facilities for having a bath on the train (either a shower bath or space for a portable bath); also latrine accommodation. No money should be wasted on ornament.

(7). ENGINEMEN'S ACCOMMODATION.

In order to ensure adequate rest for the men off duty, separate accommodation is advisable for the enginemen on the train. In South Africa there was the additional reason that the enginemen, being civilians, were better kept rather apart from the soldiers. Sometimes the enginemen were accommodated in the searchlight truck.

(8). TELEGRAPH ACCOMMODATION.

Telegraph instruments and operators should be next to the officers if possible. Each armoured train in South Africa was fitted with telegraph apparatus and telephone or phonopore or both. The telephones enabled communication to be held with blockhouses, and the phonopores with stations and sidings along the line which were usually fitted with them for railway purposes.

(9). SEARCH LIGHT AND DYNAMO.

The accommodation for this must be situated next to the engine, if steam from the boiler is used for the generator as was almost invariably the case in South Africa, the steam being taken from the dome of the locomotive boiler by a flexible pipe. The truck must be armoured to the same extent as the fighting trucks, and be provided with a few loopholes. The men working the dynamo and engine must be accommodated in the same compartment, as they may be called up at an instant's notice by bell signal from the O.C. For details of the searchlight equipment see *Detailed History of the Railways in the South African War*. A spare flexible steam pipe and a spare driving belt (where such are used) should be carried on each train.

(10). COMMUNICATIONS.

The question of means of communication between different parts of an armoured train may here be discussed.

In no armoured train in South Africa was it possible to move from one end of the train to the other along the train, nor was the need of this urgently felt, though doubtless it would be a great convenience. In most cases when the enemy were on one side of the line only there was safe communication on the protected side of the train. In trains with no protected communication between trucks, each truck, if necessary, had to do the best it could under the senior present. The train was directed from one end or another by the O.C., who could control the fire of the whole train at night by the use of his search light. The second officer usually went to the gun truck.

In a close country the advantage of through communication is much greater; but it is not easy to provide it, especially past the engine, tender, and tank. It might, however, be worth doing in elaborately constructed trains.

It is obviously vital that the armoured trains should be under perfect control of the O.C. from either of the maxim trucks. Too much importance cannot be attached to the means employed for this purpose. In the earlier days of armoured train working in South Africa O.C.s could not realize the risks they were running by not keeping all their means of communication and control in the acme of efficiency, and it usually took an accident or a narrow escape from one to quicken the perception of the novice.

The following means of communication from the maxim trucks to the driver should *all* be provided, and frequently tested to ensure efficient working :—Pull gong, operated by a bell wire ; lever fixed to engine whistle, operated by bell wire ; and electric bell, which should also be worked from the officers' truck if required. The electric bell is the most convenient for daily use, but being liable to get out of order cannot be relied on. When all else fails lamps or flags can be resorted to, but these means are very inferior and expose the signallers. A stout cord round the driver's arm will do in an emergency if the cord is not too long. It is better however for the O.C. to travel on the engine himself if communications cannot be relied on. The whistle has the advantage that the O.C. can hear for himself whether the right signal has been transmitted ; it can also be employed with advantage to give orders to the whole train. In fixing pull wires allowance must be made for the compression of the buffers, and occasional points for disconnection must be provided to facilitate shunting. Electric bell communication to the searchlight truck is also necessary.

As regards electrical leads every truck should be wired separately with draw clips, or, failing this, terminals at each end of the truck. These terminals are joined to the adjacent truck by short lengths of flexible insulated wire, easily disconnected for shunting, or for repairs if inadvertently broken. The searchlight leads should be fixed on one side of the train and the electric bell leads on the other side. All trains should have the searchlight leads on the same side to facilitate any interchange of trucks. $\frac{7}{20}$ insulated cable was used for searchlight leads in South Africa and $\frac{3}{22}$ for electric bell leads.

As regards communication between trucks, telephones or speaking tubes were tried on a few trains but I cannot say with what success. Megaphones were unsuccessfully tried. Any simple method of transmitting a written order from one end of the train to the other would probably meet the case and be the most reliable.

Finally, the O.C. must be able to apply the automatic or vacuum brakes from his post in case of emergency, the usual guard's van lever being fixed at each of the points from which the train is to be controlled. In the event of any of the levers not being fixed, the emergency brake, after the manner of that described below in connection with improvised armoured trains, should be invariably arranged for. A sudden application of the brake is to be avoided if possible, as, *inter alia*, it is liable to throw unsuspecting enginemen against sharp corners of the engine, but a preliminary tap on the lever suffices to warn everyone on the train. The protection of the brake pipes may not be possible, and in any case accidents may happen which might result in the brake being put on. To enable the brakes to be taken off without exposing the garrison, the release valve wires are led into each occupied truck, to be pulled at a given signal which might be communicated by whistle. Every armoured train must be fitted to carry ordinary train lights, and will therefore require brackets on the maxim trucks at each end, suitable for fixing either head or tail and side lights. Escort armoured trucks must also all be fitted at each end with brackets for tail and side lights.

Cycle Trollies.   Some of the armoured trains in South Africa were provided with light quadricycle trollies. These were carried on the tank, and were

used for sending messages along the line when the telephonic
communication was for any reason out of order, for conveying orders
to all troops along a section of railway, and for other similar
purposes. On account of the ease with which they are held up they
are not of much use for patrolling. In close country they would be
inadmissible, as the danger of using them on open lines would far
outweigh any possible advantages to be gained.

Every train should carry complete signalling equipment to enable Signalling
it to get in touch with any column if necessary, and to communicate Equipment.
with scouts sent out from the train or with a party sent out to direct
the fire of the train on an unseen target.

Two pair of field glasses and a telescope for the use of look-outs and
gunners should be provided.

IMPROVISED ARMOURED TRUCKS.

A special feature of armoured trains and trucks in South Africa was
the number of improvised patterns employed.

The advantages gained by being able to improvise armoured trucks
are as follows :—

The number of armoured trucks kept in reserve for special purposes
and to replace trucks during repair is reduced to a minimum, thus
releasing a certain amount of badly needed rolling stock for general
traffic purposes.

Armoured trucks cover a greater mileage in a given time than
almost any other rolling stock and are subjected to more shunting.
In consequence they require repair at comparatively shorter intervals.
The maximum time an armoured truck need be withdrawn for
repairs need not exceed the time taken to dismantle the armouring
of one truck and with it fit up another ; hence the advantage of a
pattern of truck rapidly armoured without skilled labour or special
appliances. An enormous saving in expense is effected by the
employment of an armouring consisting of materials locally available,
especially if these materials are not damaged by being used as an
armouring. Also it is not everywhere that a supply of steel or iron
plate and the necessary workshops and skilled labour for making
plated armoured trucks are available, and the *personnel* will in any case
be probably too busy with other work ; so that, unless unskilled
labour and locally available material can be used, armoured trucks
may possibly be unattainable in the required numbers.

Various materials were used in South Africa for improvised
armouring of trucks, amongst them being girders, mealie sacks filled
with earth (or better gravel), 6 ins. of gravel or stones between walls
of corrugated iron or planking, sleepers reinforced with iron plates of
all sizes and shapes fixed on as best possible, and lastly rails and
sleepers. Such armouring should be tested whenever possible, but

not in front of the men, as even though they may not be proof against perpendicular shots at point-blank range they might be good enough for practical purposes.

Of the above types, two patterns were in frequent use :— (1) Trucks armoured like the blockhouses by means of 6 ins. of gravel between sheets of corrugated iron kept the requisite distance apart by wood frames. A large number of trucks armoured in this way were employed to carry escorts, as this was the only way of cheaply armouring short trucks. Loopholes were provided, consisting either of steel plates with a small opening in the middle or of apertures (preferably **X**-shaped in plan) lined with sheet iron or wood and surrounded with the gravel filling. It will be found that the gravel tends to shake together and leave vacant spaces both along the top of the armouring and under the loopholes. To guard against the danger of this, holes are left at the bottom of each loophole, through which fresh gravel can be introduced till any cavity is filled up, and additional stones should similarly be added along the top of the armouring. Care must be taken that the stones are actually put in and that earth (which is of course useless) is not used. In South Africa a militia officer is said to have placed some of his men in a neighbouring blockhouse and ordered a few volleys to be fired at it in order to give confidence by illustrating the protection afforded by this type of work ; fortunately the occupants of the blockhouse took the precaution of lying down as the gravel had not yet been supplied to fill the frames.

Under certain circumstances rails and sleepers are ideal material for armouring trucks rapidly and cheaply. Two 10-in. jarrah wood sleepers side by side are bullet proof, as also is a 60-lb. rail. In the case of rails resting on each other, a bullet striking horizontally between two rails would probably splash through to a certain extent ; but such an occurrence would be very rare, even in the case of hot fire, and any splinters of bullets entering the truck would not do much harm.

The bogie trucks of the Cape Government Railway were about 36 ft. long. Two patterns of improvised rail and sleeper armouring were employed for different purposes on the Cape system and more particularly on the Kimberley line.

Low Pattern Rail and Sleeper Armouring.

The low pattern armouring (*Plate* VIII.) merely protected the sides of the truck up to the height of their flaps, which was 2 ft. The special fittings consisted of 6 clips, a couple of dozen wood keys fitting the section of the rail, and twelve small wood wedges,—the whole costing 30s. in South Africa. With 12 rails and up to 37 sleepers a truck could be armoured (as shown on the drawing) in one hour with unskilled labour. These trucks are useful in flat open country for the protection of working parties sent out to repair a break in the line or even for the transport of troops over much sniped sections. Fittings were kept at most large stations, so that any truck could be fitted up if required for an emergency.

The high pattern armoured truck (*Plates* VI. and IX.) required a larger number of rails and sleepers, being armoured to a height of 4 ft. 9 ins. The special fittings consisted primarily of three frames made of old 45-lb. rails, with two bolts joining the two portions of each frame at a height of 3 ft. 3 ins. from the floor level when the frame was in position; in this way a continuous loophole was provided along the sides of the truck. In addition, 6 dozen wood keys, 4 short rails each about 3 ft. 6 ins. long, and 20 ft. of 9-in. by 3-in. deal with a few spikes and nails,—the frames and all costing about £7 for labour and material—were all that was required for each truck. *Fig.* 3 of *Plate* IX. illustrates what happens in time, if the inside wedges are left out. Unskilled labour alone is required; one gang of 16 'boys' can easily fit up a truck in one day. Loopholes are provided at the ends of the truck by means of the short rails mentioned above.

In neither of the above trucks are the rails and sleepers forming the armouring in any way damaged by being used in the armoured trucks.

Both these pattern trucks have one great advantage not hitherto alluded to, but which is nevertheless of great importance and would be the more so in a close country and against an enterprising enemy, viz., strength to resist the effects of a collision or derailment. This strength is obvious when the details of construction are considered. In none of the bad smashes in which this pattern truck participated was any of the garrison seriously injured, though neighbouring trucks not similarly strengthened have been completely telescoped (see *Fig.* 2, *Plate* II.). This fact gives great confidence to the garrison and is worth striving to attain in some way in every pattern of armoured truck. These trucks were roofed with a timber framework covered with canvas or a tarpaulin, and held a permanent garrison of at least 10 men, who lived in the truck. In South Africa neither the axle-boxes nor the brake pipes were protected.

EMERGENCY ARMOURED TRAINS.

An armoured train can be improvised by using an engine with armoured cab. Some engines will always be so equipped for use in dangerous sections; but if not, it does not take long to arrange fairly good protection if sufficient plate is available in convenient sizes, and two or more of the above high-pattern trucks can then be attached. The maxims are fixed with their tripod mountings raised to the correct height for firing over the top of the armouring, the continuous loophole round the maxim emplacement being filled up with short lengths of rails, and a shield provided for the maxim if possible. The

High Pattern Rail and Sleeper Armouring.

following communications with the driver should also be provided, the fittings being kept in store.

Whistle.—The fittings required are a lever, the shape of which depends more or less on the type of the engine in use. In South Africa a lever of the shape shown in *Fig.* 4, *Plate* VIII., was employed. Stout cord and strong screw eyes are required and should be stocked beforehand. Flexible bell wire is better.

Gong.—A few gongs should be kept in store for the purpose. Bell wire or cord and screw eyes again form the means of operation.

Both the above can be fitted in a very short time.

An *Emergency Brake* can be arranged by fixing a rope round the metal fitting at the end of the flexible vacuum pipe at each end of the train and passing the other end of the rope over the front of the armouring to the interior of the truck, so that the pipe can be pulled off its socket by a heavy jerk. This simple contrivance saved several accidents in South Africa.

Accommodation for the officers and drivers can be provided in an unarmoured truck.

Ammunition, rations, coal, and water must be arranged for, a garrison detailed, and an officer with some previous armoured train experience appointed O.C.

Such a train (see *Plate* VII.) can be fitted up in a day and may be of the greatest use.

The advisability of making elaborate armoured trains in a war against a civilised power may be questioned. A highly equipped armoured train, though doubtless much more efficient and powerful than improvised armoured trains, takes a long time to make and is very expensive. These considerations would doubtless weigh in the tactical manœuvring of such a train and opportunities would be lost by the unwillingness to risk the train being cut off. On the other hand the more or less improvised armoured train, with a simply armoured gun truck containing a light 3-pr. or 6-pr. gun and spare mobile mountings or carriages for both maxims and the gun, would not be such a serious loss if isolated, especially if the armament was removed across country ; and therefore the train would probably be handled in a bolder manner. It might pay to have a certain number of this latter type of trains for use in exposed sections where the country is level and the open pattern truck admissible, the more elaborate trains being as a rule employed in situations where temporary isolation does not mean the train being captured.

GARRISONS OF TRAINS.

The garrison of a fully equipped armoured train in South Africa was limited by the accommodation of the train, which it was undesirable to increase beyond the size described above owing to the resulting loss of mobility.

A typical garrison was as follows :—

Infantry	25 (including 2 signallers)
Gunners ... .: ...	4 to 6
R.E. Search light	2
„ Telegraph	1
„ General (1 or 2 carpenters, 1 fitter, 1 blacksmith) ...	3 or 4
Medical orderly	1
Engine-drivers	2
Firemen	2
Cleaners	1
Guard	1 (sometimes a trained soldier does the duties)
Officers	2
Total	43 to 47

Every man except the medical orderly was provided with a rifle.

One officer should, if possible, be of the same regiment as the infantry, and if the gun is larger than 6-pr. Q.F. the other officer should be a gunner. The R.E. tradesmen are invaluable in effecting minor repairs on the train and in improving its efficiency and the comfort of the men by such devices as may suggest themselves to the O.C.

The medical orderly is most important; he not only attends to minor injuries and ailments on the train, but renders first aid to any casualties along the railway, the armoured train being naturally first on the spot after or during an engagement or railway smash.

If a trained soldier is employed in lieu of the guard he must have passed all the usual railway examinations qualifying him for the post.

In a specially constructed train there would probably be room for an increased infantry garrison, in which case a third officer should be appointed.

Officer Commanding.—The qualities required for an O.C. Armoured Train vary somewhat under different conditions. In South Africa unbounded keenness, energy, and dash were required to ensure the best performance of the wearisome, unintermittent, and even monotonous duties which sometimes fell to the lot of an armoured train for a considerable period, when the lack of excitement was often a sign that the work was too well done for the enemy to risk attacking a train or post or even trying to damage the railway or cross the line with live-stock. In a campaign in a civilised country a less impulsive character would seem to be best, together with much higher technical knowledge *which it would be as well to arrange for in peace time.* In any case tact is an indispensable adjunct, as also is a sound constitution.

In South Africa the armoured train afforded great opportunities to junior officers for independent command, and as there was always the possibility of achieving distinction these posts were eagerly sought after. There are undoubtedly also pleasanter moments on an armoured train. The sensation in the conning-tower on the move is at least as exhilarating as a ride on a fast motor and the effect is heightened when travelling at night with the search light. The frequent changes of scene and occasional opportunities of sport afforded pleasant breaks in the spells of hard work, and there was always the certainty of being sent where most likely to have a finger in any scrap which might be impending near the railway.

III. THE ORGANIZATION AND ADMINISTRATION OF ARMOURED TRAINS.

COMMAND OF ARMOURED TRAINS.

The fighting efficiency and the movements of an armoured train are so bound up with the technical details of its administration, and the results of mistakes likely to be so disastrous, not only to the armoured trains themselves but for the whole line of communication (*e.g.*, if the line is blocked by an accident at a critical moment), that it is imperative that the sole command of the armoured trains collectively should be vested in the staff officer responsible for their administration and efficiency. The Director of Armoured Trains* should be attached to the staff of the Commander-in-Chief in the field or possibly under different organization of the G.O.C. Lines of Communication. As regards all railway technical matters he would be responsible to the Director of Railways and he would have to be a Railway expert. If the theatre of war is large, he may have to appoint assistants or Deputy Directors—also railway experts— responsible to him for the efficiency of armoured trains on definite sections of the railway and attached to the staffs of the local G.O.C.s.

The employment of armoured trains and defence of traffic on a length of railway traversing areas under different Commandants is liable to lead to mistakes unless controlled by an officer specially detailed for this duty over a definite railway district. This Deputy Director of Armoured Trains should frequently travel along the line to inspect armoured trains and trucks, and also personally command all important concentrations on his Section. Besides being respon- sible to the Director of Armoured Trains for the efficiency of all the armoured trains and trucks in his district and for the best use being made of them, he should keep the ledgers for the equipment of each train and the accounts for coal, etc. Under this system alone is it possible to use the forces available in the most advantageous way, to secure efficiency and uniformity, to effect rapid concentrations to take advantage of opportunities, to arrange for coaling, watering, repairs and alterations to armoured trains with the least disturbance to traffic, and to *avoid accidents*. An armoured train resembles a man-of-war in that inefficiency may lead, irrespective of any action on the part of an enemy, to its destruction by accidents; such, as

---

* Bt.-Major (now Bt.-Lieut.-Col.) H. C. Nanton, R.E., occupied this position in the South African War and was attached to the staff of the Commander-in-Chief with the title of "Assistant Director of Railways (Armoured Trains)."

mentioned before, led to at least half the casualties in the armoured trains in South Africa.

Officers commanding armoured trains should receive orders from the Deputy Directors only. They must have the greatest latitude and should know best how to deal with every emergency without waiting for orders. The senior officer commanding armoured trains should be empowered to take command in an emergency, telegraphing his action to the Deputy Director and stating where orders will find him.

DUTIES OF THE DIRECTOR OF ARMOURED TRAINS.

Under the system outlined above, in the case of a large theatre of operations, the Director of Armoured Trains would discharge the duties indicated below :—

(1). Control the distribution of armoured trains among the different sections, in accordance with the requirements of the Commander-in-Chief or the G.O.C. Lines of Communications as the case may be.

(2). Frame orders affecting the working and efficiency of armoured trains generally, decide on questions of equipment or personnel relating to all trains, and obtain the necessary authority for carrying out his decisions.

(3). Appoint officers to the command of trains.

(4). Ensure general uniformity, while allowing such flexibility as may be advisable to meet local circumstances.

(5). Keep any records and statistics required.

(6). Prepare despatches, keep a general control of the accounts and ordnance ledgers, issue Army Orders and cyphers.

(7). Inspect districts, and, finally,

(8). Take command of armoured trains engaged on any very important operations involving the employment of a large number of trains.

No attempt will be made in the following pages to discriminate between those matters which emanate from the Director of Armoured Trains and those which would be initiated by his deputies, as this is of minor importance.

RETURNS.

The following returns were rendered by O.C.s Armoured Trains in S. Africa :—

(1). A nightly "Clear the Line" wire at 6 p.m. direct to the Director of Armoured Trains and repeated to the Deputy Director of the Section. This wire notified the position of the armoured train (in cypher if considered advisable). The receipt of any of the Director of Armoured Train's circulars used to be acknowledged by O.C.s Armoured Trains on their next nightly wire.

(2). A weekly diary rendered by each O.C.A.T. to the Director of Armoured Trains through the Deputy Director. This diary, besides briefly detailing movements of the train, actions, casualties, etc., described any improvements being effected to the train and contained any suggestions or requests for improving its efficiency. The Deputy Director made any comments on the margin and notified any action already taken on the points raised.

(3). Weekly state of personnel and ammunition—wired direct to the Director and a copy sent to the Deputy.

(4). Monthly return on the form shown in Appendix I., sent direct to the Director and a copy sent to the Deputy. Full details of the train, armament, equipment, and garrison were set forth in this return.

(5). Monthly nominal roll—direct to the Director and copy to the Deputy.

(6). Periodically when called for—Photo of train, and any other information required to keep the history of the train up to date in the Director's office.

ORDNANCE STORES.

As a general rule in South Africa small ordnance stores were drawn direct from any Ordnance Depôt by the O.C.A.T., the voucher containing his signature being sent direct to the Deputy Director. More important stores were obtained through the Deputy Director or with his previous authority (except in cases of emergency).

Clothing was obtained through the O.C. of each man's unit, who (as a rule) authorized the O.C.A.T. to draw direct from the A.O.D., making the requisitions out on behalf of the O.C. of the unit, to whom the vouchers were sent by the A.O.D.

Stores consigned to one train should on no account be appropriated by another without the previous authority of the Deputy Director or the original consignee.

A separate ledger was kept for each train by the Deputy Director. Maxims had to be taken on charge with all their spare parts in detail; this was just as well, as it tended to ensure that all the parts were carefully checked.

ACCOUNTS.

All accounts for services in connection with the construction and equipment of armoured trains, wages of civilian enginemen, supply of coal, etc., must be certified by the Deputy Director. In South Africa the coal vouchers were certified monthly by the O.C.A.T. before being passed by the Deputy Director. A simpler system would be for the O.C. (or the other officer on the train) to sign for coal and stores on delivery, these receipts being sent to the Deputy Director in support of the account; but it was found to be almost impossible to get a receipt for the coal from a responsible person, so that the former system had to be resorted to.

GARRISONS.

The garrisons of armoured trains are provided by G.O.C.s of L. of C. Districts under orders from Headquarters. On joining the train they cease to be under the orders of the Commandant furnishing them. The strength of the garrison must be maintained by the regiment furnishing it. A new garrison must be thoroughly instructed in their duties, especially as regards the orders for look-outs. The rules of local Commandants as regards passes for the men must be complied with or other special arrangements made, as otherwise half the garrison may be in the guard-room when the train is ready to proceed after a few hours' stop at a strange place.

One or two picked men from the garrison should be trained to work each searchlight projector.

Seven days' rations, including fuel, should be kept on the train. The trucks must be kept quite clean, especially the tanks for drinking water. Kits must be arranged so as not to interfere with fighting. Each man must have a field dressing. Generally speaking the comfort of the men must be studied as far as circumstances permit.

The men must not be allowed to expose themselves unnecessarily while the train is in the least degree liable to be fired on. Whenever the armoured train is in motion, one officer must be in the leading truck, and the O.C. incurs very serious responsibility if this is not the case. When the train is at rest at stations one sentry is required to look after the train.

The O.C.A.T. should occasionally inspect the men's equipment on the train, and should make frequent inspections to see that everything is in its place and no liquor is concealed on the train.

ENGINEMEN.

Railway Loco. Supts. should be ordered to furnish enginemen on demand if required for armoured trains. They should be picked men, so as to save the engine as far as possible in the unfavourable conditions under which it is worked ; this is very important. In South Africa some trains had to frequently change engines owing to breakdowns, thus withdrawing other engines from traffic, and as a rule the Loco. Supt. does not (if he can avoid it) give a good engine to replace one which has suffered on armoured train work. On the other hand in one case, with two sets of splendid enginemen, an engine lasted throughout the whole three years' war on the same train with only one period of six weeks in the shop for renewal of tubes. The engine was always quite clean and ready to start at an instant's notice.

The enginemen, if civilians, should be enrolled in some volunteer corps, so as to make them amenable to military discipline. Enginemen must have their rifles and ammunition with them on their engines. They must keep the doors of their engine armouring closed if the enemy are near, or at least the one on the exposed side. In no case should a door be fastened back open with wire or in any way which would need an appreciable time to shut it. Enginemen always want to keep the doors open owing to the heat, and so that they can see better.

The engines of armoured trains should be periodically inspected by specially appointed men and their recommendations notified to Deputies.

A railway guard must be appointed to each train. In S.A., where the duties were fairly simple, soldiers who qualified by passing the usual railway exam. were appointed guards with 1s. per diem extra duty pay.

Deputy Directors must keep a record of any good services of the train garrisons under them for the information of the Director. With a view to suitable recognition (*pour encourager les autres*) they should bring to notice in the proper quarter any gallant action on the part of railway servants. I can remember at least four such cases of conspicuous gallantry on my own section.

TRAINING OF GARRISONS.

Maxim Guns. —The O.C.A.T. is held directly responsible that the maxim is in perfect adjustment and condition. The fusee spring should be tested daily and the maxim fired once a week (at least twenty shots in succession). Spare parts must be carefully overhauled and the man in charge tested as to his capability of using them in case of breakdown. Care must be taken that the belts are *properly* loaded, and arrangements made for reloading belts in the case of a prolonged engagement. The reserve supply of water for the maxim must be immediately available. At least three men per truck should be taught to work the maxim.

Rifle practice from the train may be allowed to the extent of 6 rounds per man per week under the following conditions :—

(1). Firing must be personally supervised by the O.C.A.T.
(2). All posts which might be alarmed must be warned.
(3). The inhabitants or their live-stock must not be endangered.
(4). There must be no delay to traffic.

Judging distance must be practiced by daylight and by search light. In S. Africa, when a train was detailed to patrol at night with the search light, without much prospect of encountering the enemy, buck shooting was occasionally allowed on sections far removed from large garrisons, on condition that all neighbouring posts were warned of the proposed firing. This practice often turned a drudgery into a sport and afforded excellent training in scouting, judging distance, and firing by search light, such as could not have been obtained in any other way. It also provided fresh meat for the train.

Gun Practice.—O.C.s should be authorised to fire on an average about 6 rounds per gun monthly as practice, and to train spare men to replace casualties in the gun detachment. Guns, ammunition, and detachments, not commanded by a Royal Artillery officer, should be periodically inspected by one.

The whole garrison should be frequently practiced in standing to arms at short notice by day and night, including getting the search light started.

In order to make sure that all escort armoured trucks are provided with ammunition, hand signal lamps, flags, order boards, etc., and to keep a check on the strengths of the garrisons which will otherwise gradually dwindle away from men going sick or other causes, returns should, at the request of the Deputy Director, be compiled at stated intervals (about once a month) by Railway Staff Officers, these returns giving the above information regarding each escort truck at their stations.

TELEGRAPHS, TELEPHONES, AND PHONOPORES.

A compact list of diagrams should be issued to each O.C. Armoured Train showing the positions of the wires to be used for telegraph, telephone, or phonopore on the various sections. Connection is made by means of a long bamboo rod, with a metal hook at the end, which is connected by a coil of insulated stranded wire to the instrument. The rod is easily hung on the correct wire by means of the hook. The telegraph or telephone should be hitched on whenever an armoured train stops, a man being detailed for this duty, and the connection should be maintained till the train moves off. All trains in a section should be ordered to come on if possible at certain fixed hours every day. Messages which cannot be sent direct to another train should be sent to the most central station, to be forwarded when next the train comes on the wire, and should be telegraphed direct if it is important to make sure of delivery.

In the Transvaal, certain telegraph transmitting stations were held responsible that each kept in touch with all armoured trains in its section, day and night, advising the next transmitting station at once if an armoured train left its section. In this way armoured trains could be communicated with or could send messages with practically no delay. The armoured trains had to help keep in touch.

Telegraphs, telephones, and phonopores are maintained by the Director of Army Telegraphs, who provides telegraphists as in the case of any other military telegraph station.

Each armoured train should carry a few telegraph stores for repairing small breaks, and at least half a mile of cable, as the first thing to do at a break is to get one telegraph wire through some-how.

A telegraph instrument hitched on between two stations is liable to disturb the working between the two stations, and usually necessitates the re-adjustment of the instruments to enable the signals to be read. Armoured trains should endeavour to minimise any inconvenience caused in this way.

Phonopores.—The phonopore has the advantage that it can be used on the same line and at the same time as telegraph working, except that speaking cannot be heard during the actual transmission of a Wheatstone message. When there is little or no telegraph work going on, conversation can be carried on for 150 miles. With a fair amount of telegraphic work, 50 miles can be worked.

A military buzzer makes it impossible to hear, and either the phonopore or the buzzer must cease working. For this reason columns coming in to the railway must be ordered not to use buzzers on the railway line, as the armoured trains can in such cases transmit any messages through their telegraph offices. In case of need it is well to remember that a buzzer can communicate with a phonopore and *vice versâ;* also a phonopore can communicate with an ordinary telephone; but the two instruments cannot call each other up. (However, by breaking in on a conversation one can generally manage to get through in time). It does not matter if the two phonopores or buzzers are on different wires on the same line of poles, as communication is attained nearly as well by induction. About 15 to 20 phonopores per 100 miles will be as many as can be worked without interfering with each other too much.

To ensure efficient working, a definite procedure is necessary. Each station has its own call on the phonopore buzzer, generally a letter of the alphabet in morse. The phonopore calls of the armoured trains in S. Africa were " A," " B," " C," for numbers 1, 2, 3, armoured trains respectively, and so on, but preceded in each case by the letter " I." This made a very distinctive set of calls. When desiring to call up a station, listen first on the receiver to ascertain whether anyone else is using the line. If not, call up the station you want on the phonopore buzzer at intervals till the station answers by repeating its own call. Then give your own call and place the receivers to your ears. After finishing the conversation return the receivers to their hooks. If, while you are talking, somebody else calls up without having previously listened to ascertain if the line is engaged, he should be warned off by a quick succession of dots on the buzzer, or answered and asked to keep off or whether his message is very urgent. If you find the wire engaged when you want to send a message which is urgent compared with the conversation being carried on, break in on the conversation and ask the others to come off the phone till you have passed the urgent message. At times there is a great rush on the phone; but if the above rules are understood, there should be no difficulty about getting the proper precedence for urgent military or train messages.

The maintenance of phonopores is troublesome, but extra attention is less trouble in the end. In order to keep the instruments in good working order, long-continued calls which use up the vibrator battery should be avoided; and persons not concerned in any conversation should be made to keep off, as if they listen it uses up the speaking battery, and run-down batteries are one of the most frequent sources of trouble. The instruments should be kept free from dust and rain. The adjustment of the buzzer will require frequent attention, and spare platinum contacts should be carried on each train. A fuse, or carbon lightning arrester, or both, should be fixed in the circuit, in addition to the small arrester usually fixed on the instrument. One spare phonopore for every 10 or 12 instruments should be kept to replace instruments under repair. On lines where there are few trains, armoured trains can often facilitate the proper maintenance of phonopores at posts by taking the linemen from station to station on their tours of inspection or repair. It should be hardly necessary to add that any defect must at once be reported to the lineman.

Special Arrangements.—On the occasion of a " drive " or a special concentration of armoured trains for any purpose, a system of phonopores may prove invaluable if suitably organised. The special measures required are—

(1). An orderly within hearing of each phonopore at posts or on stationary armoured trains, day and night, to prevent the slightest delay in attending to calls.

(2). The use of the phonopore to be strictly limited to urgent military and train messages.

(3). A continuous note on the buzzer to be a signal for all conversation on the phone to cease at once. This signal only to be used by the officer commanding all the armoured trains or, in the event of an extremely urgent message affecting military operations, by armoured trains and officers commanding posts. When used, it is followed by the call of the person with whom communication is desired.

(4). All concerned should know where to find the O.C. Armoured Trains.

(5). The use of the military buzzer must be prohibited by stringent orders.

In the same way it can be arranged temporarily for telegraph messages from armoured trains to receive precedence over all others at the central office during important military operations on the railway. At the conclusion of the operations, when most of the armoured trains become telegraph offices for the columns, a big rush of work must be arranged for.

In all messages the O.C.s Armoured Trains should send the number of their train in words and not figures, as in the latter case mistakes can very easily occur.

PROTECTION OF TRAFFIC.

The simplest way to protect traffic along a railway is by a line of posts not more than $\frac{1}{2}$ mile apart, the nature of these posts depending on the strength and character of the enemy likely to attack the line. If of suitable strength, the daylight running, at least, of traffic should be perfectly safeguarded. Owing to the number of troops required the above method is not always feasible, and the problem more usually resolves itself into making the best possible arangement with the means at hand.

In open countries with limited traffic, some form of convoy system would probably form the principal feature, especially as its flexibility lends itself to adapting the defence of the traffic on the different sections of the line to the liability of attack on each section, thereby enabling the maximum value to be obtained from the troops available. The convoy system as employed in South Africa has already been outlined, and some of the details of working will be dealt with further on.

When posts at frequent intervals do not exist, and a regular convoy system is impracticable or not considered to be justified by the chances of attack, armoured trains can afford a very fair protection to traffic by patrolling over the sections allotted to them and convoying trains over the most threatened part of their beat. This method is of course much less reliable than a proper convoy system in that a great deal is left to chance, whereas in the latter system the traffic is, if necessary, limited to suit the escorts available.

In South Africa on unguarded sections of the line, not usually liable to molestation by the enemy, the military situation occasionally rendered it advisable to take some slight precautions. On such occasions the first thing done was to obtain the authority of the G.O.C. of the District to suspend night running over the doubtful section of the railway as a temporary measure to lessen the chances of a smash up due to the operations of one or two men. When the risk becomes sufficiently small, night running should be resumed, subject to the right of Commandants of posts to detain a train if considered advisable with due regard to the contents of the train. On the other hand it may be necessary to attach a small escort—say one armoured truck—if small parties of the enemy are liable to be met, and eventually to start the convoy system if the District is sufficiently threatened.

Suspension of Night Running.

Convoys and escorted trains should not run at night as a rule. In the case of blockhoused lines, trains were not invariably run at night; but when the enemy are fairly inactive, unimportant trains may be allowed to do so subject to the above right of Commandants. This also applies to trains timed to run in daylight but running late. Night running must of course be suspended on such sections as armoured trains are operating on. If daylight running only is allowed, when regulating the running hours of trains to suit the varying seasons of the year, due regard must be paid to the great trouble and slight disorganisation involved by an alteration to the time-table. When night running is unsafe, any trains which may have been benighted should stable only at garrisoned posts. Civilian drivers have been known to refuse to run at night when the enemy were believed to be in the vicinity ; but I have never known a driver refuse to run a train through when it was considered important that it should go.

Intelligence.   It is evident that the convoy system, and much more so any less comprehensive system of protecting traffic, can only be consistently carried out when reliable intelligence can be obtained of the presence and movements of any bodies of the enemy within striking distance of the line. For this reason the closest touch should be maintained with the Intelligence Department. Armoured trains themselves can collect a good deal of information from posts along the line and from gangers, and should, whenever feasible, carry scouts to send out and gain touch with any parties of the enemy known to be approaching the railway. Any intelligence gained should be wired direct to the Intelligence Department, to Commandants of posts concerned, and to the Deputy Director. Every train should be provided with good maps.

Patrols and Night Watchmen.   In S. Africa before the railways were blockhoused, natives were employed to assist in giving warning of any attack on the line at night. This they were very well fitted to do, as their senses of sight and hearing were keener even than the Boers'. Two extra " boys " were attached to each ganger's length (5 miles). Their duty was to patrol the line at irregular hours at night and report at once any sign of the enemy tampering with the line. A permanent watchman was also posted night and day at all the larger bridges and culverts (down to 30 ft. span) or deviation points, etc., which were not guarded by the military. These natives were all provided with lamps and flags to warn trains if necessary.

When the blockhouses were installed, the patrolling had naturally to cease, though it was still desirable for railway reasons when trains ran by night, it being the custom for the ordinary gangs to patrol the line during storms in case of a washaway. During bad storms at night on blockhoused sections, traffic was suspended till daybreak. In any case the ordinary gangs examined their lengths twice daily, when not sniped, and would report anything unusual or any spoor of the enemy to the nearest post or armoured train.

Other Precautions.   Another means of obtaining early notice of the line being tampered with at night is to insist on the telegraph being tested hourly during the night between stations, any interruption or partial interruption to be immediately reported to the nearest armoured train if accessible.

Certain other precautions are also advisable :—All concerned on the railway should be warned not to talk about the movements of trains in the presence of strangers, or in fact of anyone except the actual railway staff who have to carry out the arrangements.

Arrange that no food stuffs, cash, or other stores useful to the enemy are left by the railway at ungarrisoned stations in the vicinity of the enemy. This is particularly necessary where every endeavour is being made to starve the enemy out.

On lines where the trains run at slow speeds, as was the case up the steep grades of the South African railways, each train should have one truck, with vacuum brake disconnected, behind the guard's van, to avoid the train being brought to a standstill by the enemy riding up behind and pulling off the brake pipe. This rear truck should be a low one, so as not to obscure the side lights of the van. The tail light must be hung on the rear truck.

DETAILS OF THE CONVOY SYSTEM.

If there is not sufficient escort to provide for a daily service under the convoy system, trains may have to be run on alternate days only. Mineral trains and empties may be allowed to run unescorted, if it is impossible to escort all trains and inexpedient to stop any traffic. Unescorted trains should run singly. With the convoy system there is a block nightly (or on alternate nights as the case may be) at the terminal stations of sections, and it is of course impossible to get off both convoys simultaneously in the morning. The convoy on the most threatened section should be sent off first. Extra sidings should be put in at the terminal and principal crossing stations. As the batch of trains in the convoy naturally takes longer to complete a journey than a single train—for instance, each train having to wait till all the others have watered—every possible delay is to be cut down. Various expedients help this. The first portion of each convoy should take the traffic to and from intermediate stations. The second portion should contain the passenger coaches. The load of all engines should be reduced slightly, so as to enable the trains to conform to the regulations as to distances by increasing the pace if necessary. Checks which will necessitate any train of a convoy stopping on a steep grade should be avoided whenever possible.

In the convoy system the train in front is responsible for not getting too far ahead of the train next following, and the train following is responsible for not getting dangerously near the train next in front. The train preceding the armoured train will be apt to run on too far ahead unless this practice is checked. In open country the regulation distance was 400 to 600 yards. If the trains do not keep in touch, the escort, being split up, is nearly useless instead of each part mutually supporting the rest. A train if left behind might be easily cut off by the enemy. In close country trains must travel closer together but move slowly, whereas in open country they can keep rather wider intervals and go faster. To avoid chance of accidents when halting, each train of a convoy must come to a standstill 100 yards clear of the preceding train. In South Africa on first starting the convoy system it was difficult to get the drivers to adhere closely to the distances laid down, but after a time the system worked very well and smoothly.

Orders for Look-Outs.

The look-outs on the armoured train and armoured trucks escorting a convoy have important duties to do, and their orders should be posted in a conspicuous place in every truck. Similar orders, so far as they apply to them, are issued to all enginemen and guards on the section. A copy of the orders issued on the Kimberley section in South Africa is given in Appendix II., to indicate the nature of the orders required. In connection with these orders, although an error on the safe side, it must gradually be impressed on the look-outs and guards that the red flag should not be shown to following trains unnecessarily. For example, the regulation interval is not so indispensable going up hill as down hill or on the level; and if a train is stopped on a steep incline, serious delay may be caused. With intelligent running the intervals between trains will be found to increase going down hill and decrease going up hill. When any train in a convoy slackens speed, in addition to the red flag being shown from the rear truck, the driver should blow his small whistle to attract the attention of the drivers following, who may be attending to their engines at the time and not see the flag.

The look-outs detailed to watch the line (*vide* Appendix II.) should also look out for spoor of the enemy. If the ballast appears disturbed, the look-out should keep his eyes open for spoor on either side of the line, as the enemy may have tried to obliterate the traces of their crossing. Men should be told off to specially study definite sections of the line, so as to be able to stop the armoured train before each bridge at night if required to do so, or to say whether any spoor is fresh or old.

The above points chiefly affect the railway technical side of the convoy system. The following notes are concerned more with the military precautions taken.

Military Precautions.

The armoured train is not to run first in a convoy and should follow, not pilot, any single train it may be escorting; if the armoured train is disabled by a mine, the whole convoy may be captured, and it is also easier for an armoured train to protect the convoy in the position indicated.

Sometimes in South Africa an armoured truck used to be pushed in front of a train. Drivers object to pushing trucks as their view is somewhat obscured and loss of power is caused. As a matter of fact, although apparently tactically a better position, there was the disadvantage (unless the train was closely following another one, when the truck might as well be attached behind the preceding train) that such trucks were unprovided with cow-catchers. Moreover it is just as well that the escort should not be in the most likely position to suffer from mines. Latterly, if two armoured trucks were attached to one train, one was placed immediately behind the engine and the other behind the van.

No special trains must be run by the traffic department without the consent of the Railway Staff Officer, as he has to see that escort is provided. One armoured truck is not much use against a determined attack.

If the line is specially threatened and an attack on a convoy is anticipated, all O.C.s Armoured Trains will be warned and the escorts correspondingly strengthened. If mines are expected, the leading train must push two or three loaded trucks before the engine in order to explode them. These trucks must not be so high as to obscure the view of the driver. Special care must be enjoined in carrying out the convoy regulations, trains must be kept well in hand going down inclines, and large culverts and bridges must be specially examined before the passage of trains, either by gangers or by the leading train, preferably the former.

The O.C.A.T. is responsible for doing everything possible with the means at his disposal to protect his convoy. If attacked, the alarm is given by a long blast on the bass whistle, repeated by all the trains. The O.C. must endeavour to see all his convoy safely to the next post in either direction, after which he may devote his whole attention to the enemy if desired. Under ordinary circumstances it is hardly worth while for the O.C. to delay the convoy in order to return and tackle a few snipers. If the line is pulled up on both sides when attacked, the convoy should close up in the best position for defence, and should hold out till relieved. If the line is found to be slightly damaged, it can be repaired by the armoured train with the help of the nearest ganger. If found badly damaged in front of the convoy, the O.C. should wire for the breakdown train, giving full particulars of the damage done ; and should return with the convoy to the next garrisoned watering station, after which the armoured train can go back to the break if required.

A specimen set of orders for men in escort trucks, additional to the "Orders for Look-Outs" already alluded to, will be found in Appendix III.

The country may be of an open nature, but with crops high enough to conceal an enemy close to the line. Such crops must be razed for at least 1,000 yards to render the convoy system at all secure.

THE TACTICS OF ARMOURED TRAINS.

The tactics to be adopted by an armoured train in action cannot be laid down beforehand for all conditions any more than can be done in the case of other troops. It must be expected that if a train is attacked, it will be at one of the points on the line at which it can fight least advantageously. O.C.s Armoured Trains should take every opportunity, when patrolling the line, of becoming acquainted with the positions near the line which might be taken up by the enemy, by visiting such positions and noting their weak spots. It may be possible owing to curves on the line to enfilade such positions with searching fire if not at close range, or to bring converging fire on the position by dividing the train, or the gun and one maxim truck may be kept out of rifle range and the other maxim truck taken in to closer quarters. The armoured train must withdraw from artillery fire if the latter cannot be quickly overcome and kept down, unless vital considerations necessitate the train remaining and chancing the consequences, in which case the enemy's aim can be disconcerted somewhat by frequently changing the position of the train.

Communication should be maintained if possible with the next garrisoned post. This may be effected sometimes by using the engines of the convoy trains, each with an armoured truck from the convoy, these engines to patrol the line between the armoured train and the post. An officer should, if available, be sent with each engine.

Posts along the line are usually provided with rockets as well as telephones. An armoured train should at once proceed to the spot indicated on receiving a signal by either of the above methods.

When a party of Boers wished to cross a blockhouse line, fire was opened on the blockhouses from all points while the party was actually crossing the line. Under similar circumstances, armoured trains should remember to look for and fire on the party actually crossing.

When ambushing a section of the line with the assistance of a few infantry, the procedure in South Africa was to place sentries in pairs or groups of three at 400 to 600 yards interval along the railway, and detail an armoured train in support for every 3 to 8 miles. Each armoured train had a definite section which it was not allowed to leave under any pretence whatever. The arrangements for ensuring this are described later in connection with the notes on "Drives." The sentries may be either dropped from the armoured train or they may be made to march out so that the movements of the train may give no clue to the enemy as to the section ambushed. The sentries should be in position before it is quite dark. To deceive the enemy the train may pretend to drop sentries on sections which are to be left unambushed. The troops from convoy armoured trucks can be used for ambuscading duties at night if required, the O.C. Armoured

Train being responsible for their being attached to the convoy trains next morning. When standing on the main line on these or other similar occasions, at least two sentries should be posted from the armoured train ; they will keep close to or on the train.

" DRIVES."

The officer commanding the armoured trains on the occasion of a big "drive" should be stationed near the telegraph, telephone, or phonopore, at a fixed central point and not on an armoured train. He can then receive information and transmit orders with a minimum of delay. He should be responsible for all the railway arrangements on the section of operations, and may possibly be told also to issue the necessary orders to the troops along the line, as they can only be moved by rail under his arrangements.

On being informed of a proposed "drive" and of any extra armoured trains temporarily detailed to his section, the following preliminary arrangements are necessary, secrecy being maintained as long as possible.

Assemble trucks of coal and engine stores at convenient sidings for armoured train engines to refill from without leaving their sections. Arrange also for all tanks for watering locos. to be kept full, and also for full tank trucks to be kept where required to save armoured trains coming into a depôt for water. The tanks at all posts will have to be filled up just before a "drive." As armoured trains carry one week's reserve rations, no special action is usually necessary in this connection.

Arrange for all the escort trucks of the section to be concentrated where most likely to be useful. The garrisons may be employed out of the trucks if necessary.

Arrange for sufficient mounted or cyclist orderlies for the use of the O.C. Armoured Trains if he is likely to have to communicate with other departments at his station.

See that blockhouses or posts all have rockets for calling up armoured trains quicker than by the usual signal of three shots in rapid succession passed all along the line.

Decide on the plan of action. It depends on the relative strengths of the railway lines and driving columns whether the *rôle* of the armoured trains is to effect the capture of the enemy or to drive them back on the columns. In the former case, the railway being the stronger line, all the trains would probably lie low so as to lure the enemy towards the line. In the latter case they would patrol with search lights flashing at intervals to give the impression of a large number of trains and bluff the enemy back on the columns. Care must be taken not to throw the light on the blockhouses.

The armoured trains will probably have to help distribute the parties for the intermediate posts between blockhouses, and perhaps ration the troops along the line, or even supervise the construction of pits for the intermediate posts. The main point about these pits is that the earth obtained from them is thrown at the end of each pit to protect the occupants from stray shots from the blockhouses. The pits should enable fire to be opened on the enemy whichever side of the line he may happen to be. The distance apart of the pits depends on the troops available ; but should not as a rule exceed 200 yards, even if only four men are then available for each pit.

Arrange to cancel the ordinary train service as may be necessary. A certain amount of military traffic for the columns may have to be worked through specially. One or more good Railway Staff Officers should therefore be drafted to the section at the points where the columns are due to concentrate after the drive. The traffic on the section of operations is best worked by the officer commanding the armoured trains from his central post by telegraph or telephone orders on the "Train despatching" system, the ordinary system of working being for the time being suspended. As far as possible each train, including special trains of all sorts, should have a written order directly from the O.C. Armoured Trains. Failing this, his telephone orders should be written down by a responsible person and handed to the officer, if any, in charge of the train and to the driver and guard.

If it is necessary to run a special train on a single line during a drive, each armoured train should be told to allow the special train to pass it at that end of the section nearest the approaching train. The special train should run at fast speed over each section. In this way each section is covered by its armoured train all the while as it can dash out if necessary any time prior to the arrival of the special at the crossing station, leaving a man to explain matters and hold the train, or it can follow the special quickly as soon as it has passed.

Arrange for a reserve of gun and S.A. ammunition for the armoured trains, also for a spare armoured engine fitted with a flexible steam pipe for the searchlight engine. An extra officer or two should be detailed for the armoured trains, in case additional trains are improvised or to replace casualties.

When the drive is about to commence, combined orders should be issued to all the armoured trains. Until experience has been gained most of the following points would probably have to be included :—

Orders to Armoured Trains.

1. Allot to each train a definite section.

2. Each train to place a red light at each end of its section one hour before dusk, a man being left in charge to keep the lamp burning. In rare cases he may be allowed to conceal the light and only show it on the approach of a train.

3. Each train to place three railway fog signals 10 yards apart, 600 yards inside the red lamp at each end of its section. The train must keep between these sets of detonators.

4. O.C.s of trains would also have to understand that if the enemy try to cross the line at a particular point, the trains of adjoining sections may help with their search lights by illuminating the ground in front of the blockhouses of the section attacked, such illumination being effective for two or three miles. They must in any case look out for an attempted crossing in the section for which they are responsible, as the first attack may be a feint.

5. Trains must hook their phones on whenever they come to a stand, and should make a special point of doing so at certain notified hours.

6. Information *re* trucks of coal and engine stores; also water and rations if necessary. Before counting on coal or water, enquiries should be made as to whether they are still available. Economy of water is to be enforced everywhere.

7. During the day, in the absence of special instructions, armoured trains should carry out any rationing, etc., for troops at intermediate posts.

8. All intelligence to be at once wired or phoned to the O.C. Armoured Trains at a notified central point.

9. An officer to be always on duty in each armoured train. As far as possible he should remain within hearing of the phonopore when the train is standing.

10. Warn armoured trains of the position of any posts away from the railway but within range.

11. For special arrangements as to telegraph and phonopore working see the section on telegraphs, etc.

Very few orders are necessary for the troops along the line :— Orders to Posts.

(*a*). Each post must remain in its trench till relieved, one man if necessary being sent for rations and water to the nearest post provided with them.

(*b*). It is vital to economise water. N.C.O.s in charge of posts are held responsible that any water intended for the columns or armoured trains is not tampered with.

(*c*). The alarm is to be passed along the line by a prearranged signal, such as three shots in rapid succession; at night the post attacked must also fire a rocket.

Several points have also to be considered with reference to the arrangements immediately after the conclusion of the "drive." Surplus armoured trains will usually be sent out of the way to watering stations, leaving their telegraph offices, if necessary, where most needed.

Prisoners must be collected from the columns and brought in under the escort of an armoured train, and steps taken to ensure the proper people being ready to take them over on arrival.

All the extra men between posts must be brought in early to central stations to save water. The line of posts will also probably require water and rations, especially the former.

Arrange to collect the sick, etc., from the columns.

Finally cancel the special arrangements for the working of the telegraph and telephone and also the restrictions on traffic. The block you have caused by your operations will probably have more or less disorganised traffic and the supply of rolling stock for hundreds of miles.

Traffic Arrangements.

In most parts of S. Africa the telegraph stations on the single line of railway are a considerable distance apart, and the traffic is worked under a somewhat elaborate system by which trains are arranged to cross each other at intermediate sidings between telegraph stations. In some cases there are as many as three of these intermediate sidings, and the crossing arrangements are liable to become somewhat complicated. Trains are also allowed to follow each other, if necessary, at 20 minutes interval. The authority for a train to proceed is a written order duly signed by the station master at a railway telegraph station. This order carries the train to the next telegraph station, unless other trains are to be crossed, when the order only holds good as far as the first place where a crossing is to take place; a fresh authority being obtained from the train coming in the opposite direction. To avoid accidents these crossing arrangements must be rigidly framed and observed, and this involves a definite knowledge of the movements of all trains concerned some time in advance of their happening. With armoured trains such foreknowledge is not to be counted on, and it must be carefully considered, as regards each section of the railway, whether any special traffic arrangements facilitating armoured train movements are admissible without running undue risk of accidents.

It will in all cases be found practicable to allow armoured trains to work "Station to station" and not on a prearranged time-table, thereby insuring freedom of action and secrecy. This only meant in S.A. that drivers and guards were not to expect to be notified of any crossing of an armoured train until they saw it on their train order.

Arrangements can also be made for facilitating the "blocking" of a section while an armoured train is in it, in which case the armoured train can move as it likes while it is in the section. In a close country like England, with comparatively high speed traffic, the "absolute block" system must be adhered to, though this would not be much disadvantage owing to the double line being available in nearly all cases, and also because there are practically no intermediate sidings and the distance between telegraph stations is so short. In flat and very open sections, where the view usually extends for a considerable distance along the line, thus giving an additional safeguard, the arrangements shown in Appendix IV. were adopted in South Africa as a result of long enquiry and experience. The regular traffic in this case was carried out in daylight only, and usually ran in convoys, so that the conditions were very favourable. Such arrangements would only be applied in a close country at great risk. It would be preferable in the latter case to increase the number of railway telegraph stations during extensive armoured train operations. In some parts of S. Africa arrangements were made that an armoured train might closely precede any train, travelling in virtue of the order carried by that train.

Ordinary head and tail lights will always be displayed by armoured trains, except in sections blocked and in possession of an armoured train for patrolling, when the O.C. can please himself.

Each O.C.A.T. must be in possession of a copy of the railway traffic regulations, and must understand and obey them except in cases of grave emergency, when the O.C. is held personally responsible for the results of any action taken. If any railway traffic regulations are broken owing to exceptional circumstances, an early telegraphic report must be sent by the O.C.A.T. to his Deputy Director of Armoured Trains. Should a train in action or otherwise have to back against its "line clear" order, it should blow its bass whistle, and at night display its search light and in any other way warn possible following trains. Armoured trains must not, without very special reason, delay ordinary trains. It is better, however, to delay a train than to run risks of accidents. Complaints by the railway authorities as to the infringements of railway regulations by armoured trains should always quote the number of the train and be sent by wire, so that the circumstances can be investigated while the matter is fresh.

Tact must be employed in all dealings with the railway officials and servants, and it must be remembered that it will take time for them to get accustomed to the special conditions attending military operations.

During special working the "distant" signals may in some cases be converted to "stop" signals, if necessary to facilitate station work and give additional protection to trains standing in a station.

Engines of armoured trains should be washed out at least every ten days. A good rule is to wash out on the first chance after the sixth day; and if the engine is not washed out by the twelfth day owing to the exigencies of the service, a telegram should be sent to the Deputy Director with a view to special arrangements being made if possible for relieving the engine. Engines and civilian enginemen on armoured trains are of course independent of any Loco. section. Repairs must be undertaken in any shed or shop on the written demand of the O.C.A.T., which may support the account passed for the service through the usual channel.

When the line is blocked for armoured train operations, no armoured truck or part of an armoured train is to be left on the main line for any purpose, unless protected by fog signals placed on the line 100 yards away each on side of it. Great care must be exercised in coupling up such trucks again, especially at night.

Military Orders Interfering with Railway Arrangements. The effect of military orders on railway working must always be borne in mind and given due weight before issuing such orders. For instance, suppose a train has to run over 500 miles of railway, the first 100 miles of which is threatened by the enemy. It might be considered necessary to attach an armoured truck to the train as escort. Such armoured truck would naturally not go further than the 100 miles and would then be hitched on to some train coming the other way. The result is that the train has to go the remaining 400 miles each way one truck short of its full load, thus causing a serious loss of carrying power. The least that can be done in such a case is to arrange for the armoured truck to be the smallest and lightest pattern available, so as to reduce as little as possible the useful load of the train.

Again, it might be considered necessary to keep open day and night a railway telegraph station usually closed during the night. When deciding how long to continue the arrangement it must be remembered that this involves the expense of extra staff. In the same way, if trains are ordered to be escorted by an armoured train, arrangements should be made for the armoured train to meet them in plenty of time to avoid delay.

MISCELLANEOUS.

Painting Armoured Trains. Armoured trains should be painted to match, as far as possible, the prevailing colour of the country they are operating in. In one case in S. Africa, where a train was operating in bushveldt, the use of branches to hide the outline of the train when lying in ambush proved very effective. Disguising an armoured train as an ordinary goods train by means of tarpaulins, etc., might succeed in special cases.

Armoured trains should be numbered and known by their numbers as they are less confusing than names. All the railway truck numbers on the vehicles of every armoured train should be repainted in their proper places whenever the truck receives a fresh coat of paint. In this way unnecessary confusion in the rolling stock records is avoided.

Signals. Uniform signals from the leading truck to the engine should be adopted for all armoured trains. The following signals are recommended, though they were not the ones adopted in most cases in South Africa :—

Stop	1 beat.
Forward (*i.e.*, engine to go chimney first)... ...	2 beats.
Back	3 beats.
Slower—Caution	4 beats.
Faster	5 beats.

The advantage of having only 1 beat for "Stop" is that, if the arrangements should go wrong, or the cord break at the first beat or owing to the train dividing, safety is more likely to be attained by the driver stopping than if 1 beat is a preparatory signal. Four beats is usually given before the 1 beat for "Stop." If the latter comes without warning it should be treated as an urgent signal.

Each armoured train should have half-a-dozen signal rockets, one **Rockets.** to be sent up if engaged, two if assistance is required. Before search lights were provided, some of the armoured trains used to carry magnesium rockets for illuminating the ground if the presence of the enemy was suspected. If such rockets are employed, all concerned should be notified that they do not necessarily mean that the train is engaged.

A local cypher should be employed by armoured trains for their **Cypher.** nightly wires or other communications not with other departments. Each train must also have the Army cypher to communicate with the Intelligence Department, Staff, Columns, and Posts.

Careless use of the cypher must be guarded against. The name of the place in the nightly wire of armoured trains should, if sent in cypher, be included in a message of several words, and not sent singly. With a simple cypher as used in South Africa the key is given away by a message like TRRNQ KLDRW LZZZZ sent from Deelfontein, especially if the office stamp of that station appears conspicuously on the message! In such a case it would be as well to mis-spell the name slightly or wire in cypher that the position is, say, five miles north of the station where the message was handed in. The "Playfair" cypher, or any other cypher in which the letters are cyphered in pairs, is much more reliable, but takes a long time and requires great care in its use.

Orders must be issued to all concerned that no improvised armoured **Unauthorized** train may be placed on the line except after previous reference to the **Armoured Trains.** Deputy Director of Armoured Trains.

Stores of material for repairing the railway and telegraph, including **Line Repair** timber for temporary railway bridges, must be kept ready at suitable **Materials.** centres, and efficient arrangements made for rapidly assembling a construction train. If damage to the line is imminent, the material may have to be kept loaded up in trucks; and if frequent, regular permanent construction trains will have to be fitted up.

APPENDIX I.

ARMOURED TRAINS, RETURN FOR THE MONTH OF ....190...

No. of Train.	Armament.	Ammunition.	Garrison.	Truck and Engine Numbers and Description of Train.	Remarks.
	Search Light. Phonopore. Sounder. Vibrator.	......Total S.A.A. on Train. ......per gun. ......per rifle. ......Shrapnel Complete. ......Common ,, ...Case shot ,,	Gun Detachment. R.E. ,, Infantry Escort. Telegraphist. Lineman. Signallers. Electricians. Med. Ord. } Enginemen. Guard. } Details.	Engine .... Class.	2nd in Command, ... Regt. Section on which working.

............190...

...................................Regt.

Commanding No............Armoured Train.

N.B.,—The original of this Form was foolscap size.

APPENDIX II.

ORDERS FOR LOOK-OUTS ON ARMOURED TRAINS AND TRUCKS.

(To be communicated to the look-outs by Officer or N.C.O. in charge, and copy hung in each armoured truck.)

1. Each truck is to be provided with 1 hand signalling lamp, 1 red flag, FLAGS AND and 1 green flag. The lamp to be always kept lighted when the truck LAMPS. is on the main line after dark.

2. Two look-outs to be on duty in each truck whenever it is in motion. LOOK-OUTS In leading truck one man is to be told off exclusively to watch for ON DUTY. obstructions on the line and warn the driver as may be necessary. He is to be stationed at the front end of the truck and will give warning on the driver's side of the train. The other look-out should watch for the enemy. He is to be stationed on the fireman's side of the train.

3. Except when the train is between station signals, the look-out of a truck RESPONSI- pushed in front of the engine is responsible for giving the driver notice of BILITY OF LOOK-OUTS. any obstructions on the line as if the driver was unable to see anything.

4. When the driver is required to slacken speed or proceed with caution CAUTION owing to cattle, etc., on the line, or the train being too close to the train SIGNAL. in front, or on approaching a station, or from any other cause, a green flag must be shown by the sentry or the caution signal (4 pulls) given on the bell or whistle or other means of communication.

5. The stop signal on the bell or whistle (1 stroke) is to be given and STOP SIGNAL. red flag shown at once if the points are set the wrong way, or the line is damaged in any way or culvert blown up, or if there should be any obstruction on the line such as live stock, stones, or trolley, or if troops should be crossing the line in front, or if a red flag is shown from a train in front.

6. A red or green light is to be shown at night instead of the flag. SIGNALS. Lamp or flag signals to be shown on the driver's side, but in cases of urgency the other sentry should also endeavour to attract the attention of the fireman.

7. The driver is responsible for having head and tail lamps on the TAIL LIGHTS. armoured train. These must be lighted at dusk unless O.C. gives orders to the contrary. The sentry is responsible for seeing that these lights are kept burning when in use.

8. When escorting trains look-outs should call the attention of the DISTANCES Officer or N.C.O. in charge of their truck, when the armoured train is getting WHEN ESCORTING too far ahead of the following train or if the trains behind are separating TRAINS. too much. On the level the interval should be 400 to 600 yards and should not at any time exceed 1,000 yards, except at night, when the trains should run at intervals of a mile unless the enemy is expected when they should all go at the usual interval but very much slower.

REAR TRUCK.   9. In the rear truck one of the look-outs should be detailed specially to watch following trains. He should show a red flag or lamp, in addition to the fixed red light on the rear of the train, to a following train when his train commences to slacken speed, or is going to stop, or wishes the interval to be increased between itself and the next train for any reason.

If waved it is a signal for the following train or trains to go back. But the rear train must be the first train to go back, and the intervals between the trains must be allowed to increase, and on no account must the armoured train start setting back until the interval between it and the next train is at least 600 yards. Care must be taken not to wave the lamp or flag unless the following train is required to set back.

A green flag or light is a signal for the following trains to come on.

These signals should be passed back from train to train.

APPENDIX III.

ORDERS FOR TROOPS FORMING GARRISONS OF ARMOURED TRUCKS ATTACHED TO TRAINS.

1. The troops in armoured trucks attached to trains are under the command of O.C. Armoured Train, if there is one escorting the train. If no armoured train forms part of the escort, the troops in the armoured truck take orders in case of attack from the senior officer on the train.

2. Two men are to be posted as look-outs and relieved hourly throughout the journey. The rest of the men are to be ready to stand to arms at any time. Whenever anything suspicious is reported the whole garrison is to stand to arms.

3. To avoid firing on our own patrols or on inhabitants, troops in armoured trucks commanded by a N.C.O. should not, except in very special cases, open fire, unless fired on or unless the armoured train or some other part of the escort commanded by an officer opens a heavy fire. It must be remembered that occasionally a shot or two is fired from the armoured train as a signal to our patrols to send a man to the train. Such shots must not be taken as a signal to open fire.

4. When attacked, if the train is brought to a stand owing to the line being cut or the vacuum brake pipe being hit, the garrison of the armoured truck is to hold out until relieved, taking special care to economise ammunition so as to prolong their resistance. A man in an armoured truck is at a great advantage compared with a Boer in the open, and an armoured truck should be held against greatly superior numbers.

5. On no account are men to sit on the edge of the truck. They must not expose themselves at any time more than they do when standing on the floor of the truck.

APPENDIX IV.

ORDERS FOR ARMOURED TRAINS CROSSING ORDINARY TRAINS.

Except in case of emergency, armoured trains patrolling in any section must be at telegraph stations in time to avoid delay to ordinary trains, unless previous arrangements have been made on the telegraph instrument or phonopore with Station Masters at telegraph stations each side, and clearly acknowledged by them, or unless such arrangements are noted on the Order held by the driver of the armoured train. All such arrangements made by the train whilst in the section should be made on the telegraph instrument whenever possible in preference to the phonopore, as a record is then kept of the messages passed.

No ordinary train will be allowed to leave the telegraph station on either side until the armoured train in the section has notified its arrival on the siding where it will cross the ordinary train, or has notified the Station Master concerned that operations have been completed and that it is about to start for the siding where a crossing has been arranged. In the event of a failure of the instrument and phonopore on an armoured train, the latter will faithfully carry out any arrangements made; and failing such arrangements, will come to the nearest telegraph station to cross trains or to make arrangements. O.C.s Armoured Trains will be careful to notify Station Masters when they have arrived at sidings where they have arranged to cross trains, or, if delay is thereby saved, when they have finished their operations and are about to start for the crossing place.

LIST OF ILLUSTRATIONS.

TEMPORARY LOW-PATTERN RAIL ARMOURING.

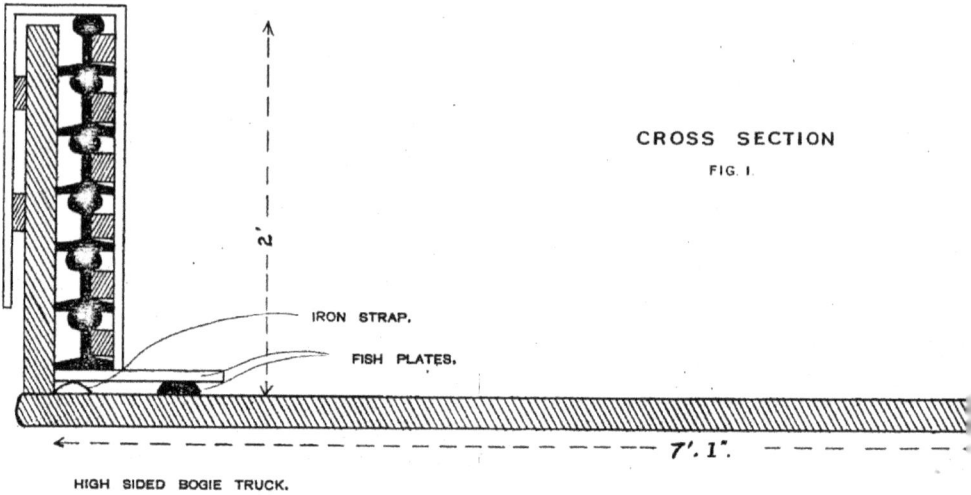

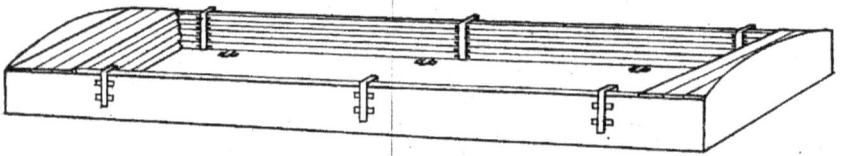

CROSS SECTION
FIG. I

2'

IRON STRAP.

FISH PLATES.

← — — — — — — — — — — — — — — — — — 7'. 1". — — — — →

HIGH SIDED BOGIE TRUCK.

GENERAL VIEW.
FIG 2

PLATE VIII

WEDGES

OF WOOD.

OLD PATTERN LOW SIDED BOGIE TRUCK.

ROOF OF ENGINE CAB.

FRONT
OF
CAB.

3"

1', 8."

1"

½"

2'

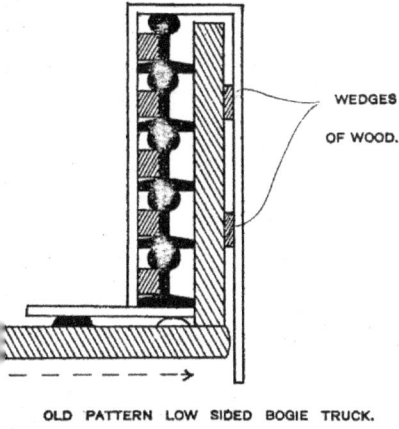

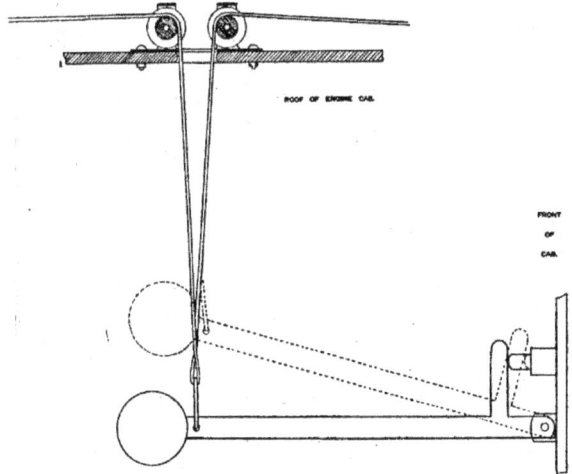

SKETCH OF WHISTLE LEVER

FIG 4.

SCALE ABOUT ¼

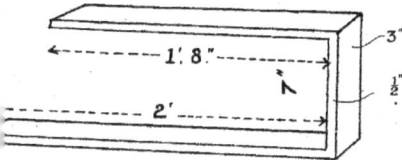

SKETCH OF CLIP

FIG 3.

HIGH PATTERN RAIL AND SLEEPER ARMOURIN

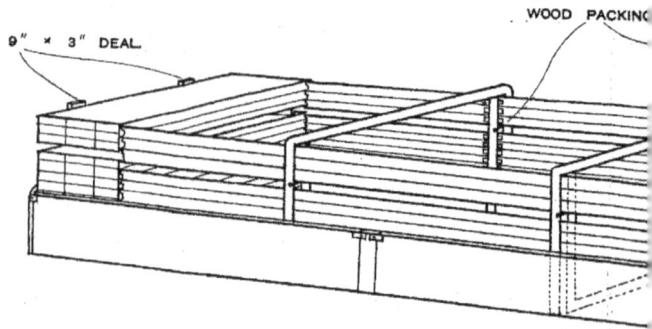

9" × 3" DEAL.

WOOD PACKING

GENERAL V

FIG 2.

30' RAILS.

7' JARRAH SLEEPERS.

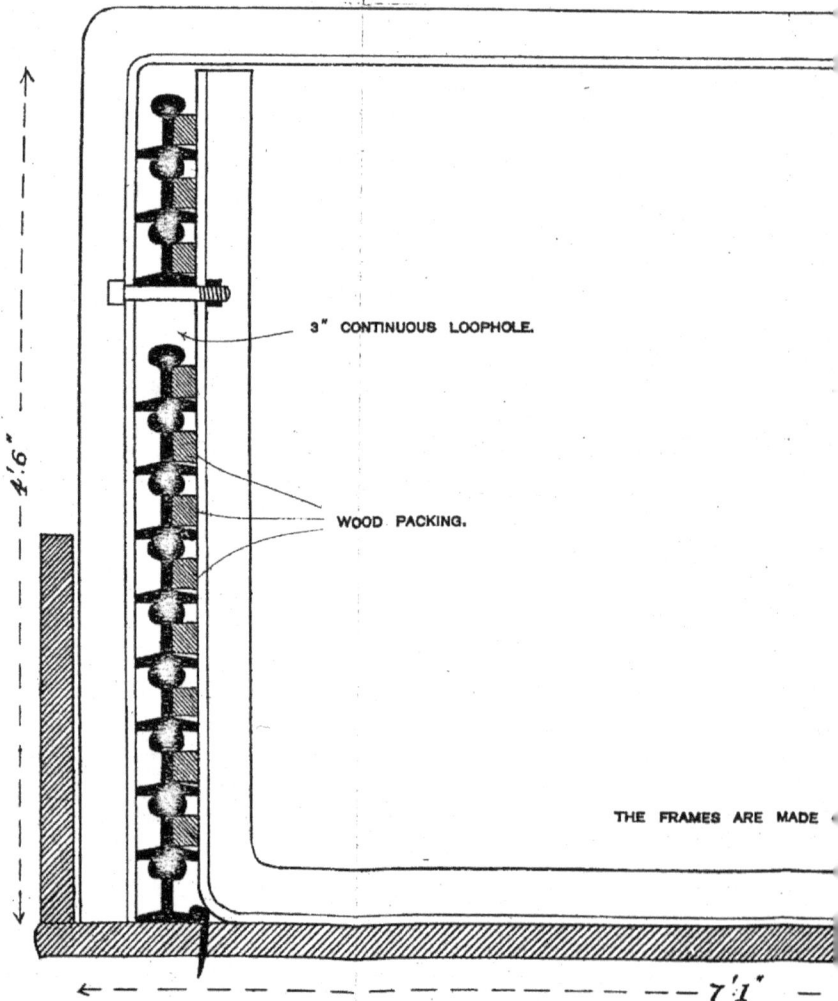

4'6"

3" CONTINUOUS LOOPHOLE.

WOOD PACKING.

THE FRAMES ARE MADE

7'1"

SECTION THROUGH TRUCK
FIG. I.

PLATE IX

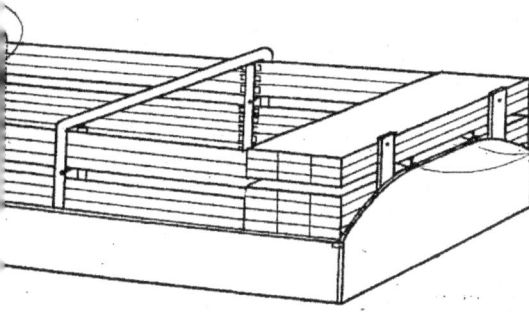

SHORT LENGTHS
OF RAIL TO
MAKE LOOPHOLE.

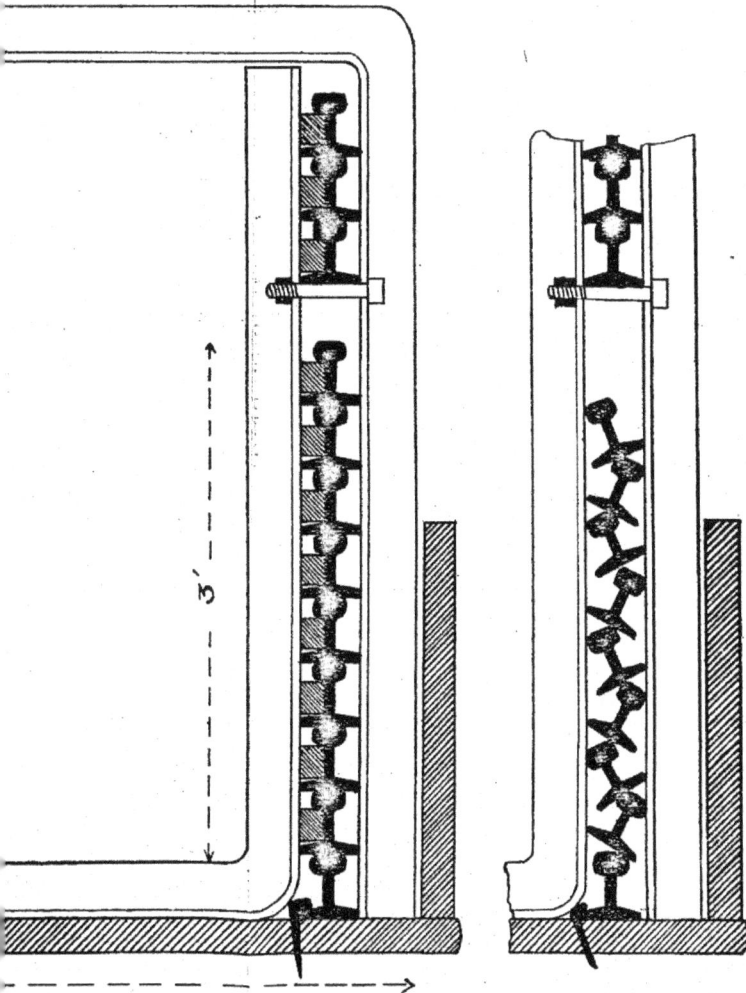

3'

FIG. 3.